100 Practices for Healing
During Times of Loss

SELF-CARE
for Grief

NNEKA M. OKONA

ADAMS MEDIA
NEW YORK LONDON TORONTO SYDNEY NEW DELHI

DEDICATION

To my dear friend Precious C. Williams and my Aunt Francesca "Nneka" Okona-Kalu: May the memory of you both continue to inspire us and guide us as we live. And to all who have grieved, and all who have lost: May you find hope, comfort, ease, validation, and softness within these pages to move forward and rebuild.

Adams Media
An Imprint of Simon & Schuster, Inc.
100 Technology Center Drive
Stoughton, Massachusetts 02072

First Adams Media hardcover edition August 2021

ADAMS MEDIA and colophon are trademarks of Simon & Schuster.

For information about special discounts for bulk purchases, please contact Simon & Schuster Special Sales at 1-866-506-1949 or business@simonandschuster.com.

The Simon & Schuster Speakers Bureau can bring authors to your live event. For more information or to book an event contact the Simon & Schuster Speakers Bureau at 1-866-248-3049 or visit our website at www.simonspeakers.com.

Interior design by Julia Jacintho
Interior images © 123RF/lovelava, vivalentino

Manufactured in the United States of America

2 2022

Library of Congress Cataloging-in-Publication Data
Names: Okona, Nneka M., author.
Title: Self-care for grief / Nneka M. Okona.
Description: First Adams Media hardcover edition. | Stoughton, Massachusetts: Adams Media (an imprint of Simon & Schuster, Inc., 2021. | Includes index.
Identifiers: LCCN 2021013722 | ISBN 9781507215937 (hc) | ISBN 9781507215944 (ebook)
Subjects: LCSH: Grief. | Psychic trauma. | Self-care, Health.
Classification: LCC BF575.G7 O33 2021 | DDC 155.9/37--dc23
LC record available at https://lccn.loc.gov/2021013722

ISBN 978-1-5072-1593-7
ISBN 978-1-5072-1594-4 (ebook)

CONTENTS

INTRODUCTION ... 4

PART ONE
A Framework for Grief and Self-Care ... 6

Chapter One: *Understanding Grief* 9
Chapter Two: *What Is Self-Care?* 21

PART TWO
Exercises to Care for Your Grieving Self ... 30

Chapter Three: *Physical Self-Care* 33
Chapter Four: *Emotional Self-Care* 67
Chapter Five: *Mental Self-Care* 105
Chapter Six: *Spiritual Self-Care* 143

ADDITIONAL GRIEF RESOURCES ... 182

ACKNOWLEDGMENTS ... 184

INDEX ... 187

INTRODUCTION

All of us encounter grief at some point in our lives. This grief might come from the loss of a loved one, a dream that must be let go of, a career path that is no more, a big move far from the community you've cultivated, a relationship that has run its course, or routines disrupted by unforeseen circumstances. There are countless ways to grieve, and no one's experience is the same. But one thing that is always true, no matter the type of loss, is that it changes you. Grief rattles you to your core. And self-care—giving yourself the things you need physically, emotionally, mentally, and spiritually—can serve as a vital lifeline during these difficult times.

Self-Care for Grief serves as a tool for peering within and discovering what it is *you* need in order to heal and move forward from your own grief. You'll find self-care suggestions for your physical, emotional, mental, and spiritual wellness. You'll:

- Tune in to the wisdom of your body
- Enlist emotional support
- Plan a vacation from grief
- Create a goodbye ritual
- And more

Some activities are step-by-step guides. Others are less prescriptive and give you room to make them your own. These activities also act as a springboard for exploring and discovering what self-care will look like for you in totality. If you've never explored self-care before, expect that incorporating it into your life will be fully transformative and incredibly healing. The chapters that follow dive deeper into both grief and self-care, so you can make the most of this transformation.

Throughout this book, take what resonates and build toward a more nourishing life. Honor your grief at every turn of the page. Accept that it exists—that it is here, and that it has changed your life forever. And that better is coming.

PART ONE

A Framework for Grief and Self-Care

If you're reading this book now, taking in these words, grief is known to you. Maybe you're reflecting on past losses that have become fresh in recent days, weeks, or months. Or perhaps the rawness of a loss has newly entered your life, and you're trying to find a way to deal with the immediate pain—to just cope in the meantime. You're in the right place.

In the chapters that follow, you'll find deeper grounding on the topics of grief and self-care. In Chapter 1, the different forms of grief are discussed, along with cultural norms and rituals for grieving, ways that grief can show up in your life, and how some people get stuck in their journey through grief. Chapter 2 is all about self-care, including its historical framework and what self-care is and isn't. You'll also find an overview of the four main types of self-care to help guide you in the activities and healing work that will come in Part 2. Go slow with these opening chapters. Let yourself have time to digest what you're reading. Divide your reading into chunks, if that's easier, versus reading it through in one go. Settle in; ready yourself for the healing that is ahead.

Chapter One
Understanding Grief

Loss touches every person on this earth in its various forms. It is an inevitability—an often unexpected upheaval that shakes up our world and demands we reintegrate the version of reality we formerly knew into a new version. In this shift one thing is made clear: There is nothing predictable whatsoever about loss and the grief that follows. And there are often certain losses that bring us to our knees, forcing us to wrestle with losing love, hope, and/or certainty in their wake. Grief happens when someone we love passes, of course, but it also happens when we lose a long-held dream or a friendship; it can be the result of a job loss, or even when we move away from a place we called home. These are all losses. And they can all encompass grief.

In this chapter, you'll delve into grief more deeply. You'll explore how it can look, what holding grief—and rituals to commemorate it—may include, as well as how grief can impact you moving forward, and different cultural traditions for honoring grief. There may be no other topic as complex as grief, but this chapter lays the groundwork for your own understanding as you navigate through the rest of this book and use self-care as a means of examining, holding, accepting, and healing your grief.

How Grief Looks

To know grief, to experience it, is to know a multitude of things. Multiple things are indeed true when it comes to grief. Grief is sadness. Grief is unbridled rage. Grief is disbelief and the inability to accept a loss that has shattered and forever altered your life. Grief is cycling through acceptance of what you've been handed, and being stunned at its impact over and over again until you're exhausted by the emotional rollercoaster ride. Grief is making on-the-fly adjustments as you grapple with loss and a new reality. Grief entails mental and emotional shifts.

Grief is all of these things and none of these things at the same time. That is because grief is an individualized experience. It doesn't look one specific way, and it doesn't feel the same for everyone. Though it would help to simplify things, there will never be one core expression of grief and loss. As diverse and varied as your life experiences are, your grief will be too. And how you hold that grief, and how it manifests for you personally, is varied as well.

Holding Grief

The first ninety days of teetering through grief are often touted as "early grief": days when those who are grieving find themselves encountering many numbing new truths. Early grief is disorienting and is best compared to ambling through a fog. Cognitive abilities are dimmed. Mental processing takes longer than normal.

Early grief follows certain norms for what it means to grieve and hold grief, especially for those bereaving the death of loved ones. Funerals, memorial services, candlelight vigils, and the like exist as ways to commemorate our loss when it comes to death. We gather in community with those who are grieving with us, because it is in community that we have support, and together we can relish the love of those we have lost. The grief that follows those early days is no less profound or searing, of course. The earliest manifestations are simply of note because they mark an abrupt transition into an unknown: life after loss and all it may entail.

Despite these common support practices and memorials, holding grief can take us on a twisted road of emotions, thoughts, and actions. And often we may feel rushed to fully accept our loss and to move on as quickly as possible. Those feelings can come from pressure we put on ourselves, messages we interpret from those around us, or from societal and cultural expectations (more on this later). So, pressures, messages, and expectations aside for a moment, how do you hold your grief in healthy, healing ways?

You hold grief by encouraging those around you who are also grieving to take their time. You hold grief by not judging yourself when you find that you are the one who is grieving; you remind yourself of that same acceptance and support you offered to others in their time of need. You hold grief by fostering more honest discourse about how grief impacts everyone, and how you can count on loss to be as much a part of your life as change. Because grief and loss don't discriminate. No one can escape being impacted by loss in some form, whether big or small.

Grief in Society

You are not supposed to dwell in your grief. When you've lost someone due to their death, or when any other loss in life makes itself known, you're not supposed to grieve for long. This is what society at large commonly hammers into your psyche with thundering immediacy. The goal with any loss—and any expression of grief—is to skip into the future, as far as possible—to integrate whatever lessons are to be learned, whatever wisdom to be gleaned, and to move forward swiftly. You are not to be sad. And you are certainly not to express your grief openly. You are to be stoic, happy even, and exhibit signs of being okay and unaffected. This is the culture of grief—a culture that both denies the realities of grief and prods people not to feel or connect to the losses that change them in fundamental ways. And it is a culture that unfortunately robs us of the depth of honesty that could happen if open conversations about grief and loss were allowed. We will all lose things. We will all lose people we love too.

To make matters worse, in our society there are no tried-and-true methods for honoring losses beyond those caused by death. There are no ceremonies or rituals that are respected as healthy ways of honoring different kinds of grief—grief over a breakup, a lost job, or a relocation away from a beloved community. We simply lack cultural traditions that might help us move through the impact these other losses have on our lives.

Grief and Mortality Traditions

Unlike other types of loss, death is associated with many traditions throughout different cultures. These traditions are cemented into communities, informing their members about what it means to grieve. While some traditions are similar across many cultures, others are unique to certain parts of the world. There are also key differences in Western traditions versus other popular traditions in other cultures.

Grief in Western Tradition

Western tradition supports grieving families in a few prescribed ways. Beyond the standard funeral (sometimes with an open- or closed-casket wake prior to the burial), a notable way of supporting those in grief is to offer food. Once word travels within a community that a loved one is gone, friends, neighbors, and others start bringing meals to the grief-stricken. The idea is that while everything else might ache, at least there is the comfort of food and sustenance—one less thing to worry about.

Unfortunately, funerals and food offerings are typically where grieving begins and ends in Western tradition. The grief then becomes a solitary experience—one to move on from as swiftly as possible. In contrast, grieving in many other cultures around the world happens communally and over an extended period of time. Read on to learn more about these communal traditions.

Grief in Jewish Tradition

Judaism commemorates death through the practice of *shiva*, the Hebrew word for "seven." Through a week-long period, family, friends, and all those connected to the person who has passed (and is believed to have transitioned into the spiritual realm) journey through what it means to grieve. This practice immediately follows the burial of the loved one. Shiva is not merely a suggestion within Jewish faith but a moral requirement. In those seven days following the burial, the grieving family—spouse, children, siblings, and parents—remain home. While they are home, other extended family members and friends visit to provide comfort and support. Shiva is intended to help those grieving by providing a formal structure that gives the okay to talk about the loss, to sort through feelings, and to find a dignified way to reenter the world after a quiet and dark seven days.

Grief in Ghanaian Tradition

The Ghanaian cultural tradition for grief is one of many within the African Diaspora that approaches death from the vein of celebration. Depending on the tribe—Ashanti, Fante, or Mole-Dagbon—the exact rituals may vary, though the central belief for all tribes is the importance of honoring those who have transitioned into ancestors. Like the Jewish shiva, Ghanaian funeral rites are at least a week long, but can easily be longer.

Nigerian Funeral Rites

Nigerian funeral rites are similar to those of Ghanaian tribes, with week-long celebrations that culminate in a burial. As is common within the Ghanaian cultural tradition, those who have died are typically buried in their ancestral villages, away from bigger cities.

Traditional festivities to honor the dead occur on a Saturday, after a morning burial. Dancing, dressing in black and white, singing traditional songs, and the playing of talking drums (drums that can mimic human voices) are some expected rites.

Grief in Black American Tradition

The flamboyance and flair that are prevalent in West African grief rituals, no matter the country, are reflected in Black American grief rituals as well. Though pockets of African Americans can be found in all regions of the United States, the highest number of Black people remain in the South due to the legacy of chattel slavery. Those who still live in this area are the direct descendants of enslaved Africans, so naturally those grief rituals have remained intact. This includes everything from ramping up activities to honor the dead prior to the funeral, to the care taken to dress beautifully for the funeral itself.

The Black American Repass

One crucial part of Black American funerals is the repass: a time for all those mourning their loved one to gather and share food. It is a form of fellowship and reinforces the importance of communal grieving for those who have passed on.

An open house is held at a central family member's home, where there is food, talking, and connecting. A wake is typically held at the funeral home, but can be held at the family's home as well. There is a funeral at a church, internment at the burial site, and the repass.

Grief in Mexican Tradition

Día de los Muertos, or "Day of the Dead," is a multiday holiday from Mexican cultural tradition and consists of honoring ancestors through parades, graveyard visits (to spend time with those who have departed), and, perhaps most importantly, the building of home altars. These altars, typically built on tables or other spaces, are filled with candles, as well as the photos, mementos, and favorite foods of those who have died.

Day of the Dead Celebrations

Día de los Muertos is celebrated following the Western holiday of Halloween, typically from November 1 until November 2. The biggest celebrations are in Oaxaca, Mexico.

The two decorations you'll most likely see during this holiday are bright marigolds and skulls. Participants also enjoy pan de muerto, a sweet bread traditionally prepared for the festivities.

Concluding Grief Traditions

Although there are many beautiful cultural examples of grief and loss rituals as they pertain to death, these do very little to address the long-term impact of grief. When all the funerals and rites have concluded, grief does not drift away. Nor does the grief for a loss unrelated to death simply disperse following that loss. Though you are expected to carry on with life after loss, grief remains.

The Impact of Grief

Despite social, cultural, or personal expectations that loss and grief be moved on from as swiftly as possible, the truth is that they demand attention. Both appear in our lives suddenly, and the impact they leave in their wake can be felt for the rest of our lives. Just as grief is an individual experience, so is the impact of that grief.

A common term related to grief in psychological circles is "secondary losses." The concept is simple: When your capital "L" Loss occurs, there are many other losses that follow right after. They're not as painful on the surface as that major Loss, but their impact can be just as damaging, if not more so. On a much deeper level than Losses, secondary losses illustrate how loss permeates each realm, corner, and facet of our lives.

A Closer Look at Secondary Losses

For a more in-depth look at secondary losses, what they are, and how to identify them in regard to your own losses, check out the resources in the Additional Grief Resources section at the end of this book.

To illustrate the concept of secondary losses, let's take the following example: A woman loses her long-time husband, becoming a widow. She has lost not only her life partner, but also her companion in ordinary, everyday activities. Commonplace activities, like grocery shopping or dining out on Saturday nights is forever changed. The traveling she liked to do with him must now be done solo or with someone else. There is nothing that is not touched or affected by this loss. In pondering what our loss means to us as we journey through grief, the enormity of this fact is magnified. This is why self-care becomes vital to survival.

Mental Health Challenges

Our mental health is impacted in various ways due to our Loss, secondary losses, and the grief they create. For those who are struggling to process loss and the myriad changes that this necessitates, adjustment disorder with depressed mood or anxiety is typical. Complicated grief is another common diagnosis, in which someone who is grieving gets stuck in a grief-loop without progressing forward in any healthy or meaningful way. This includes those who proceed down a rabbit hole of depression or anxiety and seem incapable of dealing with their grief. Those experiencing adjustment disorder, depressed mood, anxiety, or complicated grief may need to seek out the help of a licensed professional. Incorporating talk therapy, medication, and other methods of treatment prove to be successful in these cases.

Life and Relationship Changes

Because of the nature of grief and loss, those who stand on the edge of these experiences—or are in the midst of them—should be prepared to see everything in their lives shift with the sands. Nothing will be the same now. How you view life itself will change, and how you relate to losses in the future will as well. Relationships with everyone in your life will change too. They may be strengthened through the intimacy of the support you receive, or the relationships may be weakened or lost all together. But though change is an inevitable aspect of life, the changes that loss introduces to us can lend us new, beautiful perspectives that help carry us forward to what is to come.

New Life to Come

You've explored what grief is and what it isn't, as well as its origins, different traditional grief rituals, and how grief can impact a person in totality. Now comes the next step in your journey through loss: easing the pain and breathing new life in its wake. In the chapter that follows, you'll learn more about self-care and how revolutionary and downright healing self-care practices can be when navigating loss. Grief is a force touching everything it comes across. Self-care is a healer, helping make whole those who dare to use it to combat sadness, darkness, and the pain of loss. Let yourself be transformed.

Chapter Two
What Is Self-Care?

Self-care is a vital framework for infusing regular care of yourself into your everyday life. It can include anything from drinking water and spending time with loved ones, to setting goals and practicing meditation. Through these intentional acts, you are fueling your body, mind, and soul. And grief and self-care go hand in hand. When grieving, you often need to tap in to self-care even more regularly to sustain yourself as you heal, feeding energy reserves that are draining at a faster rate than before. You need self-care as a means to keep going each day while navigating loss. By practicing self-care, you elevate the amount of compassion you can extend inward, helping you to handle your hurting heart with gracefulness.

In the chapter that follows, you'll learn about self-care as a framework for healing after loss, and also about its earliest origins within feminist teachings. You'll explore what self-care is along with what self-care actually *isn't*. Additionally, you'll dive deeper into the four main types of self-care that are contained within the one hundred healing practices in Part 2. Self-care can be sustaining and life-changing. But before it can be either of those things, it starts with a decision—a moment where you decide to value yourself and to dedicate time and energy to caring for yourself. And during loss, community, support, and self-care can make an edifying difference.

The Origins of Self-Care

Renowned writer, poet, activist, and queer womanist Audre Lorde (b. 1934, in Harlem, New York) had a lot to say about self-care. She is famously quoted as saying: "Caring for myself is not self-indulgence. It is self-preservation, and that is an act of political warfare." She was speaking specifically about caring for herself as an African American woman. When she wrote those words in 1988—as a Black woman besieged by racism and discrimination—the idea of tending to herself was indeed a radical concept.

Reading More by Audre Lorde

Audre Lorde's *A Burst of Light: Essays* has insightful, candid reflections, which are certainly worth a read. Read especially if you'd like to gain more context for her views on self-care and why she calls it both self-preservation and political warfare.

It's important to note that self-care as a way of life emerged from Black activism and the feminist thought and teachings of writers such as Lorde. It was brought into being as something that had the power to alter the way people approach caring for themselves in a world raging with grief and loss, especially the grief and loss surrounding the hardships of the Black and female experiences.

Prior to Lorde's influential feminist writing on the subject, the Black Panther Party promoted the idea of self-care in the 1970s. This was a means of balancing against the medical racism that Black people often faced each time they went to the doctor or interacted with medical professionals. From here, self-care grew and evolved, eventually becoming the popular practice it is today.

Knowing these origins of self-care is crucial. No, it wasn't born in hashtags on social media or through pithy claims of a relaxing spa day. Self-care has always been linked to finding a way to survive and preserve yourself in the process. And knowing this means you'll be able to pursue your own care without excuse or guilt: In doing so, you are preserving yourself. You deserve this intentional nurturing.

What Self-Care Is

The whims of life demand intention. It is not enough to simply awaken with the rising sun each morning. Nor is it enough to look back on the day that has just passed, filled with reflection and remorse, as the sun sets and falls into obscurity. There needs to be a force, a guiding light, to counteract the unpredictability of life. Self-care can be that light.

To be precise, let's offer up a definition. "Self-care" is the sum of activities that aid in maintaining your physical, emotional, mental, and spiritual well-being. It is more than a one-off decision to do something kind or nice for yourself, although that is certainly always encouraged. It's a combination of all the things you do to keep yourself whole, filled, and moving in this life. In this way, practicing self-care can be viewed as a discipline: You commit to self-care and integrate self-care into your life. Even when you'd rather pivot and do something easier—even when treating yourself well or doing what's necessary to be filled feels like a chore—you choose it.

Brené Brown Talks Vulnerability

Google Brené Brown's viral talks on vulnerability, or look them up on *YouTube*; these videos are a great companion for exploring self-care. Brown also has a *Netflix* special in which she talks about vulnerability, bravery, and courage.

The commitment to taking care of yourself and treating yourself kindly and gently overrides any temporary resistance or apathy. You act selflessly in honor of yourself. This is self-care.

The Individuality of Self-Care

Self-care is also individual. It is an individual pursuit of discovering what you need, what you desire, and what your soul is calling for—of asking, sitting with, and imploring yourself to find the type of clarity and certainty that divine discernment can provide. To tap in to self-care means to be curious, and to be brave enough to ask what could provide more wholeness in your life.

An App for Bolstering Your Self-Care

Download the Shine app for self-care reminders sent straight to your phone. Through both phone texts and a full website (TheShineApp .com), Shine provides information on creating boundaries, intention, inspiration, and other subjects intrinsic to living authentically.

While grieving, this becomes even more vital for our inner search. Loss demands we get clear about how we will face ourselves and our lives going forward. The old way of living can no longer be our home. A new one must be built, brick by brick. Our care for ourselves—how we handle it and how earnest we are in attending to it—determines how those bricks stack up and fit together, constructing the foundation of our soul. Our level of self-care determines whether or not those bricks are solid and sturdy, or crooked and disposable, capable of being thrown aside with any little tug from chaos or adversity.

The Interdependence of Self-Care

Self-care is also interdependent. Yes, self-care is wholly focused on how we care for ourselves, through rituals and practices that contribute to our holistic well-being. But these rituals and practices shouldn't be performed in a vacuum. We were not intended to exist on islands all by ourselves. Community care is an integral part of self-care. By leaning on the support systems of friends, family, significant others, partners, coworkers, and neighbors, we are better off. We have others to rely on and to call on when we need extra help and nurturing beyond what we can give to ourselves. And what's more, by being open enough to ask for support, we ensure that others know that they can call on us too, should they need help. Thus, love and care become an ecosystem to be drawn from when our individual well has grown dry.

What Self-Care Isn't

Popular culture leads most of us to believe that self-care is an easy, effortless, and sometimes frivolous method of injecting "feel-good" activities into our lives: the manicures and pedicures, an extra scoop of ice cream, or that special dessert we like when we've had a bad day. It has become a consumerist, instant-gratification buzzword that has strayed far from its true roots and essential meaning. Yes, pleasurable things can be a form of self-care, depending on the circumstance. Yes, these are all activities that can be nourishing and comforting. But to limit the scope of self-care to only those things is to not give proper regard to what can be a transformative practice.

Self-care is also not static. Those needs and desires we discover for ourselves? They are always in a state of perpetual change and shifting, especially when we experience a loss. There are new insights and new things to be felt as the days pile up. The self-care we lend to ourselves at this time will have to adjust, as we have to adjust to our grief. And we have to be flexible in tweaking it as we see fit. As people, places, and things sometimes face their limits and no longer serve us, our self-care practices will need to do the same. It's up to us to be able to rectify what is no longer fitting to something more edifying.

The Types of Self-Care

As mentioned previously, there are different types of self-care, whether caring for yourself in the day to day, or while grieving a loss. The activities offered in Part 2 focus on the main four types: physical, emotional, mental, and spiritual.

Physical Self-Care

Physical self-care answers the question of how grounded you are—how present and in touch you are—with your body. This type of self-care asks what you are doing to ensure your body doesn't feel run-down, depleted, and exhausted. What ways are you allowing your body to operate with as much energy and vibrancy as possible? Are you moving regularly? And are you resting as much as you move, establishing a healthy balance for both?

The things we take within our bodies are also equally important: what we eat, what we drink, vitamins, and so on. In Chapter 3, you'll delve into different healing activities that focus on physical self-care, replenishing and nurturing your body during grief through movement, proper rest, and nutrition.

Emotional Self-Care

Emotional self-care pertains to the management and regulation of how we feel and how our emotions interact—and subsequently intersect—with our grief. It is a commonly held assumption that grief is about being seated in sadness and gloom. This certainly may be the case for some who are entrenched in loss. But grief is an individual experience and varies depending on the person in question, and room should be given for emotions to fall along a full spectrum. Those who grieve can be sad, morose, lethargic; they can be filled with guilt, rage, and relief; and they can also have other contradictory and complex feelings.

The Stages of Grief

When talking about grief, the Kübler-Ross model has often been heralded as the holy grail of grief counseling. Coined by psychologist and psychiatrist Elisabeth Kübler-Ross, the aim of this model is to describe the typical emotional patterns that those who encounter grief shuffle through: denial, anger, bargaining, depression, and acceptance. It is widely debated, however, so approach it with both an open mind and a grain of salt—decide for yourself how applicable it may be to your own experiences.

When it comes to our emotions, self-care is an opportunity to work on healing ourselves. Our self-care, however, should also be flexible; we can expect that our emotional experience while grieving will encompass varied states on an ongoing basis, and we want our self-care routine to reflect that. Chapter 4 delves into emotional self-care, offering a variety of activities as tools for compassionately holding and experiencing your emotions without judgment.

Mental Self-Care

Thoughts are thoughts are thoughts are thoughts. They exist on their own and can be concluded as just that: thoughts. And yet it is easy to veer into the territory of assuming that we are beholden to our thoughts, or that they communicate ultimate truths about life and our experience of living. But we have more power than that. We are not mere toy pieces moved about by our own minds. Mental self-care involves witnessing our thoughts as they come and being committed to not letting them rule us. Our minds are a powerful place to cultivate stillness while grieving—if we are careful to not trip into a minefield of cognitive distortion. The mental self-care activities in Chapter 5 are intended to help you cultivate presence of mind and healthier coping strategies.

Spiritual Self-Care

Spirituality is more free-flowing and less regimented than organized religion tends to be. It can involve the worshiping of a deity, but it can also involve finding inner peace and meaning within yourself, and connecting to others. Spiritual self-care is an invitation to find an inner space where you can ponder what spirituality might mean for *you*.

Online Spiritual Guides

Motivational speaker Gabrielle Bernstein and entrepreneur Marie Forleo are wonderful resources for infusing the spiritual into everyday modern life. They offer their insights via *YouTube* videos, *Instagram* posts, and longer musings on their websites.

Spirituality is all the more pivotal, of course, when it comes to grief. Grief can be an immensely groundless experience, shaking us from the certainty we once had, pulling at the roots of our lives. In peering at our spiritual selves, there are lessons to be gleaned and endless opportunities to find more intention and peace, as well as the courage to stand up in our faith against the unknown. Chapter 6 is dedicated to activities that encourage you to integrate and fuse a spiritual center in your life that sustains you.

Choose Yourself

Whether physical, emotional, spiritual, or mental, pouring energy into yourself is not only a choice but also a mighty declaration that you matter, and that you are focused on giving yourself whatever it is you need to heal. Self-care can light the way forward on this journey through loss, as the activities that follow will demonstrate. Take your time with these practices, and go at your own pace. Prepare to heal.

PART TWO

Exercises to Care for Your Grieving Self

Grief is emotional, messy, layered, nuanced, and complex, and navigating it can be a challenge. A little dose of practicality and a measured approach to healing in the aftermath of loss can make a vital difference.

In the second part of this book, you'll take the grounding of both grief and self-care you discovered in Part 1 a step further. Here, you'll find one hundred healing activities, divided into chapters based on the four types of self-care: physical, emotional, mental, and spiritual. Each activity has been designed to help you in the journey through your losses. Reading sequentially is optional. This part was written to give you the flexibility to choose which activities resonate most with you in order to incorporate them into the self-care you need now. For example, if interrupted or intermittent sleep has become an issue for you in your time of grief, you'll look to Chapter 3 for activities that prioritize more restful sleep and relaxation. This part is for you. It is your chance to take your grief, and all the losses you've faced, and cradle them with a degree of softness that you may not have ever known. It is your chance to place your healing above all else. You deserve it.

Chapter Three
Physical Self-Care

**Self-care to replenish and nurture your body
through movement, proper rest, and nutrition.**

Think of your body as a temple: beautiful, sacred—holy, even. Though time often creates wear and tear on temples, they remain whole due to the time, patience, and steady reverence given to them by the faithful. Our bodies require this same type of care and tenderness. Especially when faced with grief, which can be a destructive and destabilizing force. There is no part of us that escapes unscathed as far as loss is concerned. We can feel its weight on our chest each morning, waiting for us to awaken. Loss is that ache in our hips; rumble from our stomach; or those anxious, full-body quivers we often feel—our bodies are affected and altered by our experience.

In this chapter, you'll find tools for building up your physical strength to keep your morale steady and to center your efforts to heal in the days, weeks, and months of grieving. You'll focus on hygiene, cook a nourishing meal, stretch out stiffness, and more. As you'll see, caring for your body is the first step in caring for yourself as a whole, and it will be what you have the most capacity to mind during the turmoil of grief's earliest stages.

Embrace Movement

Are you present in your body? Moving allows you to not only experience the bliss from endorphins and serotonin, but it also serves as a centering self-care exercise that loosens the tension of loss and grief in your body—and subsequently reveals how those tight joints, back and body aches, and other tensions manifest in different parts of your life.

Steps for Building a Movement Practice

1. **Go slow.** Don't go from no exercise to running five miles every day and expect this practice to take root in your life. Take baby steps. If you're typically a sedentary person, work to include five minutes of movement into your day, whether it's a walk outside in your neighborhood or five minutes of stretching indoors. If you're typically more active, add a little more movement to your usual routine.

2. **Do what you love.** Try to incorporate activities you already enjoy doing and bring movement along for the ride. Hate being outside? Taking leisurely walks in a park or in your neighborhood most likely won't cut it for you. Tailor your movement to what makes sense for you personally.

3. **Practice compassion.** In building this new practice, accept that your consistency may falter. You are grieving. Be gentle with your expectations and not rigid. If you fall off or lack the energy due to your grief, hop back on the proverbial horse when you are ready. Don't be afraid to start again.

4. **Look back and notice what the practice gives you.**
    After practicing regular movement for at least two weeks,
    look back and see what it has given you. You should notice
    subtle shifts, tangible merits in your life, which will motivate
    you to keep going.

Grounding your day in something that becomes a habitual occurrence can be a source of comfort and healing. Think of it as a small gift to yourself, one that you can control and orchestrate. While grieving, there are so many distractions and happenings that fall out of your control. A movement ritual is something you *can* form with your own might. Frame it in this way: At a time when you're searching the world around you for reprieve from the pain of loss and the struggle of new adjustments, or you're looking to your emotional supporters for distraction, use this ritual to go inward instead of outward. After all, introspection is where much healing resides.

Take to the Water

We often think of water as being a reprieve—the site of our salvation when we want to rest. We imagine packing up our belongings in a suitcase and heading off to sit with our feet tickling the water's shore. Whether a road trip or a plane ride away, water waits for us. It waits to initiate us into exactly why it is synonymous with relaxation: a pause, a state of ease. But what if we also could look to water as a place where we could heal, where we could mend all that feels broken within us? And what if we could do that as we grieved?

Looking beyond where a sea, ocean, lake, or river ends, the horizon seems so out of reach—so far away, unable to be captured. And those who grieve, like you, know this feeling quite well. Grief, too, is limitless. There is no expiration to grief. No boundaries to what qualifies as part of grieving. Communing with water can be a means to give your body the care it needs. Take to the water. Go there.

It doesn't matter if the water of choice is a calm lake, rushing stream, or noisy river. It doesn't even matter if it's a pool, the smell of chlorine rushing past your nostrils, the slick tiles of the surface rubbing on the soles of your feet. Water is water. All water has the capacity to heal and provide a healing space for you.

What matters here is intention. Entering into water with the intent to cleanse, to honor all that grief and loss has taken from you—to find some sort of refuge in your pain that will prevent you from being swallowed whole—is what will make it effective. Head to the water, take a deep breath, and as you plunge beneath the surface, as you hold your breath, treat it as a chance to release the loss you've been holding. Release the rage. Release the tension, the fear, the regret, the resentment. Release it all like a wave shuddering over your body and loosening an immense weight.

Because in this moment, as the water sloshes over your body, touching every crevice and corner, it is birthing something new. The water is relinquishing its tender touch and providing a pathway for what is next—for your transformation from a state of grieving to a state of healing.

Loss is a sudden terror. And grief is how it makes itself known to us. But water…water is a balm. Water can be a key to feeling whole again—to being human in a way that doesn't feel like being scathed and destroyed. So let it. Let water be that for you. And allow yourself to make that determination to let water have its way with you. Let water be what it has always been—the beginning of transformation and healing.

Focus On the Basics of Hygiene

One of the key signs that someone may be depressed is when they neglect personal hygiene. This could mean strong body odor, unkempt hair, unclean clothes, or an overall lack of attention to appearance. The same can be said for those submerged in the throes of grief—especially in its earliest days. Hygiene, as basic as it may seem, can fall to the wayside while we grieve. The act of hygiene is simple, yet it gets lost in the upheaval of life after loss.

When your energy is most depleted, when you are standing at the beginning of what could be a long journey of grieving, lean on the basics. Focus on ensuring your hygiene is taken care of each day. Other than being self-care in practice, this is a form of discipline, something you can do for yourself daily. If it helps, make a checklist on your phone or on a piece of paper of all the hygiene rituals you typically complete. If using a piece of paper, put this list in a visible place you pass by often, such as your bathroom mirror, a wall in your bedroom, or on your refrigerator. Seeing these visible reminders often can reinforce the discipline you're trying to hone.

Compose the checklist of your individualized hygiene items now; include everything from shaving and practicing a skincare routine, to brushing your teeth and taking care of your hair. Life is hard right now. It will be hard and heavy for quite some time as the enormity of your loss spreads into the various containers and spaces in your life. By focusing on personal hygiene, you manage one of the things that truly is within your control and take care of yourself in the process.

Sacred Baths to Let Yourself Be

Bathing is a crucial part of personal hygiene, but there is a specialized way you can make the process less humdrum and more of a ritual you can look to whenever you need solace and peace. Grief requires tenderness, and sacred baths are one way of accomplishing this.

What differentiates a sacred bath from a regular bath is the amount of thought and intention that goes into it. When planning a sacred bath, think about the time of day you'd like to have one, the optimal moment to relax and take a time-out from life and pondering loss. Setting aside ample time in your schedule is one way to prioritize this ritual. Then there's the suds and bubbles: Do you want to go the bath bomb route or buy a special oil that creates a soothing foam?

Other materials to consider are snacks to munch on while you're in the bath, a special tea or another beverage to sip, and music. Curate a playlist of calm and chill tunes. For readers, a tray to go across the tub might be a good investment for holding a paperback or an ebook device. Candles can set a Zen ambiance, and an inflatable pillow can relax your neck once you're in the bathwater. A plastic cover to go over your tub drain will maximize the amount of water used. All these things and more can make your time soaking in solitude a balm when holding loss.

Find Stillness in Movement

Although it might sound like an oxymoron, there's another gift to be gleaned from embracing more movement in your life while grieving: that of stillness. How can you be focused on stillness while your limbs move and sway to rhythms of everyday life? Intention.

Whether it's through dance, yoga, Pilates, a leisurely jog, or a faster long-distance run—whatever activity suits you—focusing on your breath is a wonderful place to start this practice. As you breathe, focus on inhaling through your nose and exhaling through your mouth. This intentional breathwork will help you center yourself in the present moment and let the pain of loss and the looming, forever-changed future be wherever they are. As you breathe, your body moving in sync with itself, the rest of the world falls away. In the repetition of breathing and moving, a natural rhythm develops, and within that space stillness can enter.

The weight and heaviness of loss can be immense. One way of navigating the heaviness is qualifying what you feel or explaining the pain of your loss to those who act as your support during this time. You want those close to you to "get it," to understand what you are going through and the complexities you're processing. Helping others understand can be draining, however, as you are utilizing emotional energy that is already running low.

This is why stillness in movement, focusing on deep breathing as you move, can be powerful. As you move and breathe, you erect a space only for you, a space where no one else can enter or dwell. Where you don't have to explain or qualify what it means to grieve and can be at peace with what this experience is like for you. While grieving, this kind of nonjudgmental, no-pressure space to simply be is vital.

Turn to Alternative Healing Modalities

Healing can assuredly take a long time—for some, it can even be a life-long journey. When it comes to grief and loss, healing sits at the crux of all you must surrender, all you must let go of that may weigh you down or leave you feeling stuck. And just as there is no one set time-frame for when you will be truly healed, there are endless ways to face the healing that must occur. As part of your own journey through grief, look toward alternative therapeutic modalities for new perspectives on healing and physical wellness.

Chinese medicine has a lot to teach us while grieving. Take, for example, the fact that one of the first things to be disrupted when processing a new loss is sleep. In order to distill the wisdom our disturbed circadian rhythms are trying to impart, the Chinese medicine body clock divides the twenty-four-hour cycle into two-hour increments. According to the body clock, if you're waking up repeatedly at the same hour every night or notice yourself falling into a similar pattern, it is not merely coincidence.

Each two-hour increment corresponds to a part of the body—such as the small and large intestines, gallbladder, liver, pericardium, stomach, spleen, or lungs. These increments also correspond to natural elements: earth, metal, wood, fire, and water. Each body part and its corresponding element is trying to communicate to you about your body. For instance, if you are repeatedly waking up between 4:00 a.m. and 5:00 a.m., the lung zone, which corresponds with the metal element, may be telling you that your body is struggling with letting go of grief.

One way of repairing a disturbed rhythm within your body clock is to balance the energetic pathways that flow through your body, also known as your qi. Chinese acupuncture is a great way to restore energetic balance. Contrary to popular assumption, acupuncture isn't simply about pricking your skin with needles. In an acupuncture session, a skilled practitioner, certified to offer this healing modality, targets specific pressure points throughout your body. These pressure points are believed to unlock both emotional and physical imbalances, releasing tension and encouraging better flow of your qi. The experience is intended to leave you feeling unburdened and lightened.

Cupping is another alternative healing method—used primarily in Asia, but also in Eastern Europe, the Middle East, and Latin America—that may prove helpful for those grieving. This practice uses cups to apply suction-like pressure to connective tissues and muscles. The goal of cupping is to increase circulation and blood flow to areas of the body that are giving the patient issues, thus promoting the body's own capacity to heal.

There are countless ways to heal. Consider an alternative modality to assist you in your grieving journey, helping you provide the tender care your body needs and desires.

Dance to the Beat of Music

Think of the last time you went to a concert: surrounded by other concertgoers in a communal environment, singing along to your favorite songs. As you're flooded with memories, and the music plays in your head, you're transported back to that place and time. Perhaps one of these songs helped you through a difficult situation, and those accompanying emotions also come up now—happiness, sadness, relief, feeling understood. Music can be a healing balm.

During times of loss, the power of music can be used to help you tune in to your body, shed lethargy, and boost your mood during one of those heavy and hard days. Take a dance break to aid in moving forward:

1. Start by choosing an upbeat song and decide how long you want to have your dance break—for as little as three minutes or as long as seven (odd-number intervals are best, as songs tend to fall within these ranges).

2. Now dance. Move as you feel guided to move. Shake out any angst or frustration. Be present to truly feel the music as you move.

3. Scream, laugh, or cry while you're moving if you feel you need to. This experience is truly your own.

4. Once you're done, pause and catch your breath. Your heart will be racing and you may be panting. But for a moment in time, you were present, you were distracted, you were immersed in another world. For a moment, your grief did not completely hold you.

Find healing in the power of music.

Get Dressed and Be

It's been a long time since you felt like yourself. In your grief, your hair may have grown longer and is no longer regularly groomed. Instead of putting effort into your wardrobe, you likely opt for the comfiest clothing possible these days—sweats, yoga pants, or pajama bottoms with whatever shirt happens to be clean. You want to care more, and you sorely wish you did. Because if you did care, it'd be one less thing on that long list of things in your life that has changed.

Yes, grief has changed you. Your energy is zapped and finite. The things you once heartily looked forward to doing are not a thought anymore. And loss? Loss is a monster that has you speeding at full throttle toward the edge, constantly reminding you that nothing is permanent anymore. You're afraid to hope, afraid to be present, afraid to feel.

For a moment, put all of these things aside. For a moment, even if you have to muster all the energy you've been saving up for a rainy day, climb back into the chamber of the past and be your intentional self. Dig into your closet and put on that favorite outfit—the one that makes you feel powerful, confident, and in charge. And even if it feels silly or futile, put it on. Put a little more effort into your hair and face too. Take the time to do your skincare routine.

Now go somewhere. Walk to a nearby coffee shop or visit an old restaurant that has a comfort meal you like. Let yourself be the person you used to be. Just for a moment.

Relish Sacred Rest

When our lives are in upheaval, when we are thrust in the middle of great change and transition, sufficient rest is often the first thing to go. Feeling unsettled while grieving loss (and the anxiety that often accompanies it) can disrupt regular sleep patterns—causing us to sleep too little or intermittently for hours at a time instead of soundly through the night.

Loss necessitates that you intentionally pause to take care of yourself, and this especially means making rest more of a priority. Your brain is busy churning, trying to make sense of the loss, to comprehend the gravity of it all, leaving you more tired than usual. There is grace to be extended to those in your life—family, friends, significant others, coworkers, and neighbors—who are doing what they can to offer comfort, but may stumble and do or say the wrong things. And when you aren't rested, you may be unable to extend grace to those who are doing their best to support you. You need rest—more rest, even—to be okay. Grief demands it. Take your sacred rest.

Start small and spend an additional ten minutes in bed each day, with the intent of building up to no more than an hour over the time recommended by your doctor. As you lie in bed, call to mind what you are grieving, and hold the tension of how that loss feels in your body as tightly as you can muster. As you release the tension and loosen the tightness in your body by exhaling, imagine releasing and letting go of what you lost. Sit with how much more relaxed you feel. Repeat as often as necessary whenever this makes sense for you personally, whether at night when you first get into bed, or in the morning after you wake up.

Build a Sustaining Sleep Regimen

When nestled within the throes of grief, sleep can be a marker that normalcy has been violently disrupted. In the early days of loss, most who are grieving find themselves staring back at a ceaseless string of sleepless nights. This might be the case for you; maybe you find yourself rising earlier than you ever have and unable to go back to sleep, or sleeping sporadically for hours at a time.

Proper sleep is one of those corners of life that seems seductively easy at first glance. It's just sleep, after all: something that we all need and only requires us to retire into the darkness of the night. Why is it so elusive then, especially while grieving? When dealing with grief, our bodies are exhausted, and though we want and require rest, it is much easier said than done. Ruminating, processing your loss, and wondering about what the future holds: All these things can keep your mind busy and render your body restless.

You'll have to take special care to restore some restfulness in your life when other parts of your life remain up in the air and scrambled. Consider drinking soothing herbal teas before bedtime to wind yourself down. Spritz a lavender essential oil on your pillow or bedsheets, or dab it on the bottom of your feet. Ensure that your room is adequately dark, or sleep with an eye mask. Also be sure to set a bedtime routine you can stick to each night. This should include cutting out screen time at least thirty minutes before going to sleep. Taking melatonin tablets is another option, but be careful to not become too dependent on these or any other medicinal sleep aids.

Naps can be another gateway to recapturing the rest you are losing, helping you feel motivated and physically restored instead of weary and waning. The Spanish have long known about the restorative power of naps. For eons, shops and businesses in Spain have closed down for hours at a time in late afternoon. Known as a "siesta," this is a practice that you can incorporate into your own life; one that encourages you to pause daily for a rest, giving you more energy for the remainder of your day—whether your day includes work duties, cooking dinner, cleaning, or tending to children or elderly parents. Though it is less of a custom in bigger cities today—such as Madrid, Barcelona, Valencia, or Bilbao—the practice of siesta remains.

There is no better time to incorporate a morning, afternoon, or even nightly nap to keep you going than when you are grieving and sifting through loss. Determine what time of day is hardest for you to remain the most awake. Adjust your schedule to include some time to nap to your heart's content. This practice will change your relationship to rest—and by virtue, your relationship to your grief too, as lack of rest is known to increase levels of cortisol (the stress hormone) and disrupt mental acuity.

Cook a Meal to Honor Your Loss

We always need to eat. That food is nourishment for the soul is an integral truth. Like rest, when trudging through grief, eating is one of the first things to be neglected when facing the instability of our new lives after loss. Some struggle to eat enough in a given day, letting food and meals become a passing thought. Others indulge more than they usually would in an attempt to feel comforted. Both are normal for those grieving, and sometimes you may also swing from not eating to overeating or vice versa.

Turn the concept of food, nourishment, and eating on its head through a practice with intention: cooking to honor your loss. Pick a time of day, whether in the morning, afternoon, or evening. Select a meal—a complex dish requiring a recipe as a guide, or a simpler one that you can do from memory. Gather your ingredients and start the meal by setting an intention. Maybe you want to cook the favorite meal of a loved one who has passed on. Or maybe you're sorely missing the neighborhood you used to live in and where all your friends remain; cooking a meal you used to enjoy with them at a potluck or a local restaurant can prove meaningful.

The acts of chopping, slicing, dicing, stirring, sautéing, roasting, letting liquids come to a boil, and more are already inherently meditative. And with this exercise you are allowing something as ordinary as meal preparation to be more impactful, connecting you to what you lost and what remains dear.

Elevate the Self-Care

Need cooking inspiration? Look no further than *Pinterest* for mealtime ideas. Also visit Epicurious.com, which has a recipe finder where you can plug in ingredients you already have on hand.

Tend to Your Hands

Most of us neglect our hands. We look to them to hold so much in our lives, but the care we lend to them can often be lacking. Not moisturizing our hands regularly, not protecting them with gloves when handling rough or toxic materials, trying to remove things from an oven or other hot surface without oven mitts, are all common practices. They deserve better. This is especially true when grieving; as with every other part of your body, you may notice while deep in your grief that your hands ache. There are no distractions from pain during a difficult time—or at least there are fewer distractions. Whereas you may have happily missed it before, now you can feel the tension and creaking in your hands as you spend endless time on the computer typing or holding your phone texting, stuck in the same position.

Pause to care for your hands. Create a new habit of stretching them in the morning when you wake up and then again at night before going to bed. Another simple act of care is to shake them out; shake out the tension for about thirty seconds, allowing your hands to breathe and release what you have been holding within them.

Your hands cradle your world. Neglecting them means neglecting an important vessel that guides the rest of your body. Care for your hands so your hands can take care of you in the ways that you sorely need.

Elevate the Self-Care

Find your hands aching or tender at the end of the day? Purchase a hand brace comfortable enough to wear as you sleep. Opt for a Velcro adjustable hand brace if you find that helps.

Start a Craft Project

Our hands are the motor key to the rest of our bodies. They literally cradle our world and assist us in the most rudimentary tasks—and the most elemental ones too. By taking care of our hands, we can take care of ourselves and the temples that are our bodies. But while grieving, our hands can also be a tool for creating something new in the emptiness of loss.

Crafting projects fall into this category. In using your hands, you can tap in to your creativity and the stillness that focusing on a crafting project often requires. Artistry in this realm runs the full gamut: There's sewing, knitting, painting, scrapbooking, screen printing, clay making, and even rubber stamp carving. When picking a project, you can choose to focus on producing something tangible, such as a painting, scarf, blanket, or completed scrapbook. Or you can try mastering a new skill. These skills can include any number of things, like knowing which stitches or repeated movements are needed to complete a scarf, or what brushstroke or painting technique can achieve a certain effect you're looking for.

Crafting can be used to inject some newness into your home, or for making gifts for those people in your life who have offered support during an emotionally perilous time. For materials to complete your craft, head to your local arts and crafts store, or shop online. Depending on where you live, there might be locally owned alternatives. Do your research and gather what you need.

Not ready to do crafting projects out in the world among other people just yet? Look no further than online options for live-streaming and prerecorded craft classes with detailed instructions. *Skillshare*—an online platform with classes on topics ranging from photography to creative writing—is one such option. For other craft-focused websites, *CreativeLive*, *Craftsy*, and *Creativebug* are great choices. All of these sites have free trial memberships, so you can test the waters before making a commitment.

Think of this crafting project—whether you opt to knit a scarf to keep you warm during the winter months or a blanket symbolizing moments that remind you of your loss—as a ritual of remembrance. This is a chance to focus on creating, on letting your imagination and passion blossom in a beautiful way. It is sacred intent, willed in a way that allows you to give birth to something else while you nurse your grief and loss. It is an activity to hold your loss and the weight of what something meant to you before it was no more.

Integrate More Touch

If you're grieving, if your world and everyday life have become the sum of new adjustments to how loss has forever altered them, chances are you feel isolated in some way. Even those who are well supported with their losses have moments when they feel utterly alone. This is the nature of the beast: As much as we strive to be connected, no one can know exactly how this painful experience manifests for us—especially not physically.

In general, Western society is a lot more isolated than it used to be. With technology replacing many in-person activities and things we used to do in the flesh, the amount of physical contact we have with others has become less and less. And for those of us who live alone or away from family and friends, this can lead us to being starved for touch.

Studies show just how radically consented touch from those we love can increase our release of serotonin and elevate our moods. These touches include everything from hugs and kisses from our family or friends, to physical intimacy with our romantic partners.

Ask yourself: Are *you* touch starved? Has it been a long time since you were hugged or kissed? Do you yearn to be held by someone who cares for you and is present in your time of need—in your time of grief? If touch is on your list of things that would fill a need right now, ask for it. Reach out to those you feel comfortable with and express how you could use a hug or that you'd like to be held. Let them know that you need physical comforting while holding your grief.

Weighted blankets or holding a pillow to simulate receiving a hug are helpful alternatives for those who live alone or far away from loved ones. Taking time to caress your skin or hold your hands over your heart are other ways of extending self-love and comfort. Touch can be gratifying if you want it. Find a way to get the utmost amount of comfort during this difficult time.

Get Some Vitamin D

The wonders of a bright, sunny day without a cloud in sight remain unbeatable. A picnic in the park on a grassy knoll, a leisurely walk, or simply breathing in air as the sun radiates off your face simply feels good. And truly, these things are good for us on a biological level. Getting sunlight also proves beneficial to those grieving. Gamma rays give our skin natural amounts of vitamin D, which can boost our mood, give us more energy, lead to better rest, and contribute overall to a better quality of life. Think of homes or rooms without adequate natural light: Spend too much time in one and watch your energy, morale, and motivation take a nosedive. We need sunlight. The following list offers tips for getting more vitamin D:

1. **Schedule sunbathing times in your day.** Sit outdoors and set a timer on your phone for no more than five minutes. Take a deep breath and close your eyes. Feel the sun warming your skin. Visualize how you'd like the rest of your day to go.

2. **Wear sunscreen daily, even if primarily indoors.** Even spending just ten or fifteen minutes outside warrants sunscreen. Remember to use a sunscreen made specifically for your face, versus using the sunscreen intended for your body on your face, which can lead to breakouts. Sun exposure can still happen if you are not outdoors sitting directly in the sun, especially if your home has lots of sun spots.

3. **Spend more time outside to boost vitamin D levels.** Revel in spending more time in the sun for the plethora of benefits it offers. But also veer on the side of caution and avoid overexposure—dealing with a painful sunburn, followed by peeling skin, is unpleasant.

The magic of the sun is healing; it's a natural mood booster and a wonderful tool for coping with loss and grief.

Watch for Heart and Digestive Issues

The weight of grief is felt and held within our bodies. This is why physical self-care within a season of loss is pivotal. We give to our bodies unceasingly, so that this kindness will aid in rebuilding our world.

The stress and turmoil of grief and loss can wreak havoc on our bodies in ways we cannot afford to overlook; namely, heart and digestive issues. High levels of cortisol, the stress hormone, means that our digestive systems can revolt in response to an overload caused while adjusting to the change of loss. Additionally, perhaps your eating habits have changed as a result of grief, such as eating less or eating more than you're typically accustomed to. Both of these situations can affect the efficiency of your digestive system and can lead to chronic indigestion or overall discomfort.

Our hearts are yet another organ we must take care with when faced with loss, as grief can impact our cardiovascular health. In fact, studies have shown that grief can change heart muscle cells and affect coronary blood vessels, preventing the left ventricle of the heart from contracting properly. Doing regular cardio (see the Embrace Movement and Dance to the Beat of Music activities in this chapter) can aid in heart health. Priming your diet to be more aggressively heart-healthy is another way to take care of this essential organ. This may mean incorporating regular servings of leafy greens and limiting things like red meat, refined sugars, and alcohol.

This caution to be mindful is not intended to alarm you but to make you vigilant. Your body is sensitive and always speaking to you if you dare to listen. Make sure that *you* are listening as best you can, even as you grieve.

Use Physical Props to Assist in Body Maintenance

You know your body needs special tending to at this time as you wrestle with your grief. You feel it when you wake up, and as you carry on throughout your days. Self-care in the form of physical props can help you in this endeavor. When you think of props, you likely think of things that are static, that give more support. And that is essentially what physical props entail in this activity as well.

One example of a physical prop is an acupuncture mat. This mat, which looks similar to a yoga mat, has special plastic protrusions across it. Some mats come with a pillow-like cushion at one end for resting your head on during use. As with acupuncture itself, an acupuncture mat is intended to hit pressure points and body meridians to promote a number of benefits. Though these benefits haven't been officially studied in a medical capacity, according to *Healthline*, those who use acupuncture mats regularly report a reduction in headaches and back pain, as well as loosened muscles, better rest, and decreased fatigue. To use an acupuncture mat, simply lie on it for a predetermined amount of time.

Foam rollers are another prop that can help smooth out body tension during grief. They're exactly what they sound like—long, cylinder-shaped rolls made out of hard foam, which you use by gently rolling your body over. These can require a bit of a learning curve in order to use them to their fullest potential, so don't give up if initially it feels like your efforts are in vain. The versatility of foam rollers can't be overstated. There is not one area of the body that is better suited for these; they can be used anywhere, especially on those trouble spots that often plague you with stiffness and pain, including your inner thighs, back, neck, and shoulders.

Physical props are a supportive tool. They are an aid in gifting yourself the self-care your body requires—demands, even—on a regular basis. Give yourself that much. Your grief demands it.

Plant Something in Homage of a New Beginning

The earth is the cradle of creation. All natural life springs forth from the earth and its fertile soil. Flowers bloom from it. Fields of wheat and other crops rely on it in order for a harvest to be reaped, season after season, year after year. In the context of grief and loss, soil and earth remind us of new beginnings that are waiting to be claimed in the wake of what has been taken from us. We can always begin again. We can always choose to rebuild, to be reborn in new, ripe, *purposeful* soil. That is, if we make the choice to see it that way, if we choose to be open to a new perspective.

Soil and the earth serve as powerful metaphors for life after loss. There is plenty to be learned from looking toward nature; despite the devastation it steadily faces—from natural disasters to human error such as climate change—it finds a way to soldier forward. Nature is resilient, shifting, shaping, and surviving no matter what threatens to dampen or extinguish it. We have that ability too.

In looking to nature and the lessons it offers, there's an opportunity for us to actively contribute something to the circle of life ourselves. Spending time in nature undisturbed for prolonged periods of time is one great way. Hiking or leisure walking may be how you prefer to pass your time outdoors. Or perhaps picnicking in a park or wading through a stream, river, or other body of running water is more your thing. Look at your time outdoors as an opportunity to replenish yourself, take a break from the work of grieving, and bask in the here and now. There is no loss to ponder or difficulties to face in this moment.

Another way of connecting with nature in order to understand your loss and hold your grief in a more hopeful light, is to plant something that you can nurture in homage to the new beginning you are embarking upon. Are flowers your favorite thing? Instead of buying fresh ones from your local grocer or florist, try your hand at looking after your own. Or are you a home cook? Consider growing a collection of fresh herbs to have on hand for your recipes. House plants can cultivate a more serene home space, so consider adding them to your decor. Whatever plant you decide to grow or outdoor activity you choose to try, know that nature calls to you a steady reminder of what can come—and how there is hope for new life after loss.

Elevate the Self-Care

Planting and growing your own greenery can involve a learning curve. If gardening just isn't for you, contributing to a nonprofit organization that will grow a tree on your behalf is a great alternative that still beautifies the world around you.

Watch Alcohol Intake

When we are sad—when we are overwhelmed, anxious, bored, or grieving—it can be easy to pour a glass. Then another. And another. And another. Before you know it, drinking in excess becomes a pattern and a way of coping. Balancing loss and grief makes this attempt to numb the pain far more complicated.

Yes, it'd be much easier to avoid holding the despair, confusion, disillusionment, and anger you're most likely feeling right now, as you stare into the abyss where your former life's realities reside. It'd be easier to dull the ache that throbs and threatens to make you feel like you're drowning or sinking. As we know, however, alcohol is a depressant. It will blur your senses and quiet all that ails for a little while, but what happens once you're done drinking? Once the morning comes again, and all you have left are the symptoms of a hangover—a throbbing head, a scratchy throat, and the type of thirst that feels like it'll never be dampened? Your loss still remains. And it will remain no matter what you do in an attempt to outrun it.

Have a drink if you'd like with a nice meal, as you watch a movie, or when you bond with loved ones in those rare moments you feel up to it. But be careful of the urge to drink your way through the pain. Remember that your pain cannot be erased with a cocktail.

Elevate the Self-Care

Alcohol-free cocktails are always an alternative. Use a variety of juices, herbs, flavored simple syrups, and ice to simulate the experience. Look to *Good Drinks: Alcohol-Free Recipes for When You're Not Drinking for Whatever Reason* by Julia Bainbridge for inspiration.

Check In with a Doctor If Something Feels Off

You know when something doesn't feel right. When all your efforts at self-care—changing your daily habits or forming new ones—are flailing or not quite measuring up to what you fully need. When that moment of clarity arrives, when you could use a second opinion or voice of wisdom regarding tending to your body as you grieve, give your doctor a call. Make an appointment for a checkup, and talk to your doctor about your concerns.

A good place to start is to ask your doctor to order blood work. Having blood work done can point to a lot of issues that a simple hunch or deep-gut feeling may not be able to diagnose. These tests can reveal issues that need to be discussed and dealt with, such as anemia, high or low blood pressure, or high cholesterol.

Depending on what blood work or any further testing shows, your doctor can help you troubleshoot health concerns and support your overall physical self-care, or give you a referral to a specialist who may be better equipped to do so.

Your body is a source of wealth. You only have one. Work with your doctor to come up with solutions you feel both comfortable with and comforted by. Don't be afraid to ask for more assistance and insight into what might not feel quite right.

Scream to Release the Weight of Grief

Grief is a full-body experience. When processing what our losses come to mean to us, the tension of those emotions—wrath, confusion, disbelief, and melancholia—become wedged in our physical form. Our backs, shoulders, necks, arms, hands, and more hold all that we feel. After a while it becomes a heavy weight. Let's put that weight down. And let's do that through screaming.

Screaming is a way of release. It is doing the opposite of bottling up all that you are feeling, all that is churning within your body, and instead offering it back into the atmosphere from where it came.

There are multiple ways you can approach this therapeutic practice. One is the tried-and-true method of screaming into a pillow. Take a fluffy pillow from your bed or one of those decorative throw pillows from your couch. Make sure it's big enough, then scream into it. Scream as loudly as you can during this practice. As you scream, focus on all the feelings you want to release and give away.

Another approach is to scream into nature. You don't want to alarm neighbors, family, or friends, of course, which is why this method is preferable. It is a solitary experience without an audience. Go to an empty park or for a hike in an area not crowded with people. Yell as loudly as you can. Again, think of what you want to release as you do.

Other therapeutic places and settings where you can scream:

- A hotel room, in the quiet of the bathroom
- On a bench in an isolated area
- At the peak of a mountain
- In a meadow full of flowers
- In a valley as the sun sets
- On a grassy walking trail, as the sun rises
- With the company of a trusted professional (e.g., your grief counselor)

Let it out now.

Incorporate Regular Stretching

Remember physical education in elementary, middle, and high school? You'd wait and wait and wait until that time of day, whether it was in the morning or the afternoon, and change into more comfortable clothes. Along with your classmates and those who were lucky to become your friends, you'd play kickball, or try not to be hit by the sting of a bouncy rubber ball in a rousing game of dodgeball. Now, remember the one thing your PE teacher always made everyone do no matter what was in store for class that day? Stretch. Stretching is elemental for any type of movement.

The main purpose of stretching is what the word implies—stretching our limbs and muscles in anticipation of the workout they will soon get as we move. Stretching helps ensure that we won't injure ourselves during whatever physical activity we choose. We are, in essence, warming up our bodies.

There is opportunity here to turn something ordinary into a loving act of ease, solitude, and reflection, regardless of whether or not you plan to exercise afterward. Start your day with a five-minute stretch, working out kinks in your back and neck from a night of sleep. Take deep belly breaths as you stretch and long, slow exhales too. And right before bed, repeat the same actions. Try slow stretches that release the tension of sitting at a desk all day at work or commuting in a car. You deserve it.

Let Yourself Laugh

When was the last time you laughed heartily? When was the last time you laughed until you cried or your belly and sides ached from being so deeply amused? Laughter can be an act of great joy—and a time and place to connect with your childlike, carefree nature.

In addition to boosting your mood, unadulterated laughter can loosen physical tension in your body, stimulate organs (such as the heart and liver), and activate your body's stress relief. Grief introduces stress and tension to our entire bodies, so taking care of them in such a heightened emotional time is crucial.

The following are suggestions for bringing more laughter into your life as a means of easing your grief:

- Watch silly cartoons, preferably those geared toward children (e.g., *SpongeBob SquarePants*, *Tom and Jerry*, *Looney Tunes*).

- Tell jokes with friends or family members to share your laughter with others.

- Plan laughter breaks where you simply let yourself laugh with abandon for short periods of time.

- Stream a comedy special.

Laughter is medicine for our souls, but most importantly, it can introduce ease and joy into our bodies. Allow some relaxation during your time of loss with the gift of laughter.

Listen to Your Body's Wisdom

Our bodies will talk to us if we're willing to listen. And when they talk, they may either whisper like a fluttering of butterfly wings or roar like a rushing dam. One of the main things that dawns on people who start to incorporate regular, consistent movement into their lives is how disconnected they have been from their body. We all have bodies; we live in them each day. They keep us literally moving from one moment to the next. And yet it's rather easy for us to see our bodies as separate from who we are instead of an aligned essence of ourselves. For some, this disassociation is due to past trauma; when we faced real threats to our bodies in the past, we numbed this connection in order to survive. Tuning back in to our bodies will require intentional awareness.

One way of listening to your body and establishing a deeper connection is to periodically do a body scan. A body scan is what it sounds like—scanning your body for sensations and messages, slowly taking in the feelings of each body part one at a time as you sit or stand with your eyes closed. When you do a body scan, you are pausing to see what feelings may come up when there aren't any distractions. A rumbling in your stomach, a creaking in your knees, shaky hands, or a racing heart: All these things could be pointing to something deeper going on. Once you're able to identify the issues, you can then translate that knowledge into active self-nurturing.

Your body will also tell you basic things you need to do throughout the day. A rumbling stomach, for instance, could be an indication that you are hungry. While grieving, your appetite may be absent. This rumbling is a reminder to pause and nourish yourself with food. A headache could be communicating stress or dehydration. This is a reminder to hydrate and to pause to take a few deep breaths in the name of de-stressing. Interpreting these messages can be enlightening if you have the courage to be open, to pause, and to notice.

Come Up with a Health Plan

Food is the gift of life. And yet while grieving, it can either become a hassle or a source of comfort. As a common cultural tradition, neighbors, friends, or others who are close to the bereaved bring food following the loss of a loved one. As soon as the news ripples through a neighborhood, community, town, or family, food may start showing up to comfort those as they make funeral arrangements—casseroles, buckets of chicken and biscuits, sandwiches, dips, baked goods, and more to feed those who are not thinking about what to eat.

The idea is a noble one: While you are in pain, as the loss becomes more real in each moment, you're offered food. The burden of having to think about what to prepare or staring mindlessly at a stove is taken away. Giving food is a symbol of care. Extend that same care to yourself.

You may be barely eating right now, because the anxiety and stress of your loss has made you lose your appetite. Or perhaps you're over-indulging in all kinds of rich foods in order to placate the pain. Either way, you need balance. And a health plan can help you find some. Give meal-planning a chance, if you think it may be worthwhile. Batch-cook dinners or stock up on food that can be easily thrown together with little effort or premeditation. If you haven't already, consider taking vitamins to address your specific health needs. And ramp up your efforts to drink more water. Dehydration can make us feel unsettled and more irritable than usual. Combining these symptoms with grief is a train wreck waiting to happen.

More Tips for Creating Your Own Health Plan:

- **Write everything down.** Write down the names and contact information for your doctor and your grief counselor, make note of your appointments, medications, vitamins and other supplements, and include your meal plan. Grief messes with your memory; a written record in one place will help you keep everything straight.

- **Use a calendar to schedule everything.** Write down what you need to do hour by hour: when you'll eat, when you'll take medication, and when you'll do your movement practice(s). And be sure everything can reasonably fit into your schedule. The aim is to write it into reality, not to feel constrained or burdened by all that needs to be done.

- **Create hacks for yourself that can be easily repeated.** For things like meal prepping, buy glassware or plastic containers to portion out meals you cook in advance. For any vitamins or medications, keep them in a labeled, day-by-day pillbox. For snacks, portion them off in washable containers for easy grabbing.

- **Be patient.** It will take time to see the merits of prioritizing your physical health and thus your physical self-care. It will take time for you to convince your body it is worth doing. It will take time for the fatigue to lift and to feel the effects of the tenderness you are offering your physical form. Give yourself that time. And lend yourself patience in the interim.

Your health plan is a guide for helping you keep all the separate parts of your physical health in order. Look at it in that way—a way of injecting ease and organization into taking exceptional care of yourself.

Chapter Four

Emotional Self-Care

**Self-care to compassionately hold and experience
your emotions without judgment.**

Our emotions are truly the wellspring of our being. They offer wisdom, guidance, and intel we otherwise might ignore or have trouble seeing clearly. When we are in touch with what and how we feel, and when we unabashedly face both of these truths, there is an overarching clarity present as we navigate our everyday lives, in public and private. Tending to our varying emotional states is also an important part of processing through what grieving loss entails. Grieving can be an emotional tailspin of ebbs and flows, highs and lows, and random circling through the stages of grief.

However grief may look for you, one thing remains the same for us all: How we manage our emotional self-care, and how gentle we are with ourselves at our most vulnerable time, matters. In this chapter, you'll encounter rituals and other activities to help guide you toward tending to your emotions compassionately, such as asking yourself what you need, setting boundaries, and fighting grief isolation. Go slow, go gentle, go true.

Give Yourself Grace

The weight of grief and understanding of loss that you must now live with can be an enormous load. What makes loss so devastating for most of us is how unexpected it tends to be. We often live our lives expecting certain things to remain in a static state. Then loss appears, challenging that assumption, and forcing us to grapple with how fleeting and temporal most things truly are. And grief—the process of trying to integrate this new life tinged with loss—enters soon afterward. We are forever changed by this void. Just as grief demands presence in order to heal, consider bringing grace along for the ride too.

Offer these things to yourself: grace, compassion, tenderness, kindness, and patience. Life has countless ways of showing you its unrelenting callousness—how rough and brutal its experiences can be. Loss most certainly falls in this category. In choosing to be soft with how you handle yourself in the midst of it all, you extend to yourself a timeless gift.

Because here's the bitter truth: We cannot control what life brings our way. Nor can we control what or whom we lose. But we *can* control how we show up for ourselves and the ease with which we allow ourselves to heal in each unexpected moment. There is an opportunity to practice absolute love for our hearts by choosing to handle them carefully, like the precious vessels they are.

Read on to discover a practice that can make extending grace to yourself part of your everyday life.

To Practice a Moment of Grace:

1. Take five uninterrupted minutes (or as few as sixty seconds, if that is all you have to spare) for this practice. Sit down and close your eyes if that feels right. This moment is especially for you and nothing else.

2. Within your moment, inhale and exhale as slowly and deeply as possible. Breathe in through your nose and out through your mouth. As you breathe, let the cares of the day fall away. Let the weight of grief fall off you too.

3. Still breathing deeply and slowly, reflect on whether or not you've been kind or affirming to yourself today. Did grief trip you up in a big, explosive way? Did you make a mess? Did you offend someone or make those who have been supportive uncomfortable? It's okay to be at fault. It's okay to screw up. You are doing the best you can in an unimaginable situation.

4. If you have extended grace to yourself, then give yourself thanks. Tell yourself that you deserve that kind of gentleness and sincerity. Affirm yourself over and over again with warm, lifting, and encouraging words. Fill yourself up with goodness by remembering to be generous with yourself when you need it most.

5. If you have not given yourself grace, do not berate yourself. Do not be rough with yourself for not being as kind as you could've been. Instead, view it as an invitation—a future chance to work toward making that type of self-care instinctual. Where it becomes as commonplace and as automatic as breathing. And as you depart this practice, affirm the pledge of kindness and gentleness that will carry you through your day.

Honestly Ask Yourself What You Need

Grief can drive you berserk. At times, you may feel absolutely out of your mind due to the emotional highs and lows that come with the territory. For a string of days, you could be doing fine. And then a new day dawns, and you're distraught. This is just what it is. Grief is hard. It is emotionally exhausting.

But so is not getting what you need as you grieve. During a time of loss, one of the more common phrases you'll hear from everyone imaginable is "Let me know if you need anything." It's certainly well-intentioned. You've most likely shared your pain of loss with this person, or they heard from a friend or family member of yours, or saw you post about it on social media. They want to vocalize their support. But they do so in a manner that puts the brunt of the effort on you to reach out. And let's be real: Most days, you won't have the bandwidth for that. Not at all.

Try something here: Ask *yourself* what you need. What exactly is it that you need to feel supported right now? Is cooking becoming too much of a chore? Does the thought of running errands totally deplete you before you can even get in the shower? Is there an ardent need for you to talk through your loss with a compassionate, nonjudgmental listening ear? Take a moment to reflect on what could make you feel more supported and less alone.

And don't stop the self-questioning there. How does your grief feel? What color is it? Is the energy of it sad and despondent, distant or aloof, or circling around disbelief and bewilderment? Are your energy levels a rollercoaster ride depending on the day? Are nights easier? Are days harder?

Getting a pulse on how grief manifests for you specifically is an important part of tuning in to your emotional needs, helping you adjust your self-care to benefit and bolster yourself. One way of doing this is to do regular check-ins with yourself. This is similar to what you might experience in a place of employment when a manager or other supervisor schedules routine meetings to ask you work-related questions and to see how things are going for you. You need to do this for yourself and your grief. Especially when it comes to your emotional state.

If you're already connected with a grief circle (a sharing circle that provides support and community to those grieving), communities online, or a grief counselor, perhaps some of this checking-in will be inadvertently facilitated in these environments. Often when sharing with others, we feel more comfortable admitting things that we are reticent to admit to ourselves. Separate from others though, this process is still essential.

One last thing: Make this process as nonjudgmental and low stakes as possible. The objective is not to berate yourself for doing anything wrong. There is no wrong here—only a space for you to be honest about what is coming up for you, and the steps you can take to aid in your healing.

Let Yourself Feel

Our emotions are meant to be processed—translated into some sort of meaning and contributing to our growth and healing. But first and foremost, they must simply be felt. When was the last time you gave yourself permission to feel what was coming up for you emotionally instead of bottling up your feelings, intellectualizing them away, or denying them entirely? Give yourself this permission now, in the midst of your grief. Doing so will make a radical difference in the highs and lows as you cycle through the process of grief, enabling you to manage your emotions with ease, clarity, and gentleness.

Read on for some easy steps to first identify what you feel, and then how to proceed through those emotions once you do.

1. **Notice what emotions arise.** Is it anger, sadness, or confusion? Name how you are feeling; don't be afraid to look for clarity by asking yourself how your emotions are revealing themselves (for instance, do you feel more reactionary or more detached?).

2. **Be present and objective with the emotions.** Once you arrive at what it is you feel and how it is manifesting, sit with that feeling without judgment. Let each emotion pass through you completely.

3. **Notice the sensations in your body that your feelings have caused.** Where do you feel those emotions? Do you have shaky hands, a tightness in your chest, a heaviness in your feet? Let the sensations be.

It has often been said that the average emotion remains with us for no longer than sixty seconds total…that is, if we're willing, curious, and compassionate enough to witness the emotion that shows up for us, rather than fighting it or casting blame.

Enlist Emotional Support

No one can exist on an island by themselves. This is especially true when talking about grief and working through your losses. Isolation is a rather common tactic those who are grieving employ. It is easier, and, in some cases, feels better to tuck further inward rather than risk looking outward—feeling vulnerable by asking and receiving support. But in the end, cutting yourself off from others can cause more wounds and add more baggage that you will have to deal with later. Ask for help and expect to be supported as you move forward and heal. After all, this is what building connections is for: to mutually be there when in need.

Getting this emotional support, however, may require you to be judiciously honest with yourself. If you, for instance, lack the kind of friendships where you can be emotionally vulnerable, you might learn, for the first time, that your friends don't have the capacity to be supportive. Or that your friends are only able to give you support in certain ways. There are friends who are able to be there for you when you need to talk through your grief. There are friends who would be happy to sit with you in silence, because they don't have the words, but you need company. There are friends who can tend to your practical needs, such as running errands or making sure you have meals to eat. Identify which one of your friends falls into each category and then ask them for specific kinds of support.

Talk to Your Loss

As far as grief is concerned, there is so much talking to be done. But it's not talking in the literal sense that most of us know. It's talking within ourselves: talking to figure out what we need, talking to discern how we feel, and talking to reconcile what it means to be standing on the other side of loss. Talking within ourselves is one way of steadying the grip on our life when things feel like they're careening out of control. And it can help us understand where we currently stand in our grief.

If you've lost a dear person—maybe a marriage is ending in divorce, or you're experiencing the death of a loved one—talking to them out loud could be comforting. Choose a time of day when you know you'll have quiet and alone time. Make sure you're seated comfortably and light some candles in honor of this moment. And then, talk.

Close your eyes if that makes it easier to approach the conversation. Talk as if you are seated right across from this person you miss. Share with them anything you want: recent happenings, things that made you laugh, current frustrations, or exciting things on the horizon. With those who enter our hearts, even when we go our separate ways or they pass on, it is not necessarily the end. There is still space to honor what the relationship was and what it represented for you. In talking to the loss you now hold, you are honoring it in action, while also accepting that the bond is different than it was before.

If your loss is more intangible—a former way of life, or a neighborhood you once called home—the idea of talking to it might seem more abstract and strange. But the concept is the same: holding reverence for what was once meaningful. You can talk out loud or quietly to yourself about what you appreciate or loved most about the thing you have now lost. How did it make you feel? Loved? Appreciated? Whole? Reflect on these things. Once again, honor them in action, through speech.

Trudge Toward Acceptance of Your Loss

As you explored previously, the Kübler-Ross model implies that acceptance is the final stage of grieving any loss. The idea is that you cycle through all the other stages (denial, anger, bargaining, and depression) before eventually landing in a place where you can accept your loss—and the grief that comes with it—and can finally move forward with your life. If you are grieving, you probably know that grief and loss are infinitely more complicated than that.

Grieving is filled with individual nuances—such as what the thing or person meant to you, how they fulfilled an emotional need, and the quality of the relationship you had. Sometimes, people will suggest that the closer and deeper the relationship in question was, the more intense the loss. That's a presumption that is unfounded and not necessarily true. No guarantees can be given when it comes to grief. And such is the same with accepting the totality of your loss. Nonetheless, acceptance is an important part of grieving, one you should take care to continue processing.

Try not to think of acceptance of your loss as this looming, final item to cross off your grief to-do list. Instead, consider it to be an ever-changing, evolving concept that takes on a different weight as you grow, change, and heal—as the loss becomes more concrete and less abstract to you in innumerous ways.

Accepting your loss might not mean you move forward in your life in certain ways. It may not mean that you give yourself permission to try something different or start anew in some respects because your loss crushed you. It may mean you dig your heels in deeper, hoping to cling to the life you knew before everything changed. And by digging deeper, you find new resonance right where you are. Maybe circumstances in your life didn't change outright, but you did. That's still acceptance.

Listen, we all know that life goes on. The world turns. New beginnings appear whether we're ready for them or not. Grief anniversaries come and go. Acceptance then begs the question of how you will live. How will you allow this loss to change you? How can you integrate the devastation and the pain into something real? Something good? That's the challenge. That's where acceptance enters. We stop trying to turn our worst nightmare into just a figment of our imagination. And instead, we look at the horrors of what we wish never happened straight in the eye and pledge, quietly, bravely, and fearfully, that there is still life left to live. And we'll be right there to live it.

Accept That All Your Relationships Will Change

Grief is a catalyzing force. Grief has the capability to crystallize life truths that we formerly may have been too distracted or undiscerning to see. This is no truer than when it comes to the connections we have to people in our lives. Grief changes everything. It changes us—the core of who we are—so naturally it also changes how we relate to those around us and the shape of those relationships.

Some relationships will be strengthened by your vulnerability in this critical time of need. You'll find some friends show their hearts when it comes to tending to you as you grieve and make sense of loss. This will make those relationships closer. Through something as brutal as loss, you see that this is someone you can count on—not just for the highs of life, but also for the crushing lows.

There are other relationships, however, that the destructive nature of grief and loss will shatter. Some people may be unable to sit with the magnanimity of your loss. Others will have nothing but silence and distance to offer you in response. Know that these people aren't bad people: They aren't selfish monsters, refusing to show up for you due to some deficient quality in you. Their lack of support—and this fundamental change in your relationship with them—does not underscore your worth. Some people simply don't have the bandwidth to share and be a witness to your pain.

Schedule Crying Bursts

You need to cry more. Grief is asking you to cry more. Loss is asking you to make crying a regular part of your self-care.

To cry does not automatically mean you are sad. Crying is one of many forms of emotional release. A person can cry because they are frustrated, worried, stressed, overwhelmed, confused, at their wits' end, joyful, in awe, or relieved. Crying, letting the tears freely flow, means there is emotion your heart wants to express—emotion it *needs* to express.

Early in the grieving process, it's not uncommon to feel numb. For some, when we experience loss, we feel so shocked that numbing ourselves to all we are processing serves as protection. Crying might seem futile for those who are experiencing this. Which is why you will need to schedule "crying bursts"—short blocks of time devoted to crying. Schedule time to cry like you would schedule a doctor's appointment or a therapy session. Pencil in just a few minutes—or as many as ten minutes—once each week. (Even if you aren't numbing yourself, scheduling those crying bursts can create room for regular emotional release.) See how crying and having that space to release emotions that have nowhere else to go changes how you grieve.

Elevate the Self-Care

Prepare to feel lighter after the release of crying settles in, but you may feel initially drained. A hot cup of tea, a bath, or simply heading to bed are effective means of cushioning a good crying session.

Set Better Boundaries

Some shudder when they hear the word "boundaries." The term can sound big, scary, and confrontational. And for those of us who aren't accustomed to advocating for ourselves in such a direct manner, there's a reason we feel uneasy around the notion of boundaries. We've never had boundaries before, and uncharted territory is always unnerving. But boundaries don't have to be a big thing. They don't have to be scary either. It all depends on how we view them.

Look at them like this: Boundaries aren't walls that we put up in order to keep others out. They're also not rules or a means of controlling the actions and reactions of others. Boundaries are about *us*. They are about our needs and our wants. They are necessary in order to center our self-care so that we don't drown in a sea of demands from others. When we shift our thoughts surrounding boundaries to encompass this broader understanding—that boundaries are about us and standing up for ourselves—the energy of setting boundaries can feel different. The concept suddenly becomes empowering. It's about our emotional safety. And that is what you need most while grieving. You need to feel safe.

So yes, tell your parents that you don't have the capacity to run endless errands for them on the weekends because you require more rest at this time. And yes, when your close friends once again vent about issues they need advice on, share that while you'd love to listen and help, you're too drained to show up for them in that way right now. And yes, ask your boss if there can be a redistribution of work responsibilities during this period of grief: You need a lighter workload until you feel up to operating at your former level of productivity. And yes, limit your input of any triggering TV shows, movies, or other stimuli in order to not cause emotional harm to yourself. These ways and more can be boundaries you set depending on what needs tweaking in your own life.

There are also two very important things to keep in mind as you set better boundaries for yourself:

1. Expect to receive resistance or disappointment from those who have never had to ponder your limits before now. Do not allow their reaction to sway your needs while grieving.

2. Do not waver in sticking to the boundary you have set because it may initially feel "mean" or uncomfortable. The guilt and discomfort will pass. The preoccupation with how others feel about it will pass too. Your needs at this vulnerable period of time, however, will not. Let what you need drive what you do.

Contrary to popular belief, boundary work is not one and done. You will never reach a point where you are done setting boundaries, renegotiating the terms of them, remaining firm in them, or enforcing consequences when they are crossed. Boundary work is ongoing, requiring you to face what is and adjust it to what can be. And while grieving, those types of shifts are everything.

Learn How to Say No and Mean It

Saying no—gleefully, forcefully, without any remorse—will change your life. And it will also change how you grieve.

You know how grief and navigating loss have been for you personally. You know that intimately because this is your own experience. Ask yourself, when it comes to saying no, what are your gut instincts for things you no longer want to do? Or for social situations that require too much explanation about how you are feeling or how you are doing, and become more draining than energizing in the end? Circular conversations that are lacking in empathy?

Reflect honestly. And the next time you feel the no rising in your throat, and you have the urge to squelch it in order to be thought of as nicer and more agreeable—not a dreary, difficult, grieving person— think about what a difference it would make to not trouble yourself with those emotional calculations. How would it feel to say no and be relieved that you don't have to involve yourself in a rigmarole where your feelings are not being considered anyway? How would it feel to put yourself and your grief first?

Say no. Then say no some more. Say no even when you feel guilty for saying it. Say no when you feel relieved to opt out. Say no when you feel the drain coming on for something you don't even want to do. And then say no to other things you don't want too.

Your loss is asking you to be present for how you feel. Saying no more—and thus saying yes to yourself and your needs—can be revolutionizing. Saying no to what you feel lukewarm, lackluster, or ambivalent about means you have room to say yes to things that fill you up, aid in your healing, and center processing your grief in a healthy way for you emotionally. And, well, why wouldn't you want to go gallantly in the direction of that?

Limit Social Media Processing

When you're grieving, social media can be a beautiful place to find others who are grieving too. The countless grief communities that have sprung up on *Twitter*, *Instagram*, and *Facebook* have proven immensely helpful for people. These social media platforms are heartily encouraged for you to find your people—your companions in grief. Enforcing limits to your social media use as an outlet to process grief, however, is also a good idea.

It's easy to log on to social media and espouse your thoughts on how grief feels like to you. When loss is rawest and freshest, we want to tell the world of the pain we feel. The wretchedness of it demands not only to be felt but also to be shared. And so that's what many of us do, unwittingly. And in some cases, inappropriately.

Self-expression is always a good idea—when it is kept sacred. When you feel the compulsion to ramble on social media about grief often, consider what your intentions are. Do you feel isolated and need connection during this time? Turn that energy into finding a grief circle or other means of communication where there's a higher likelihood that you will be heard and understood. Needing to simply express your feelings? Try journaling or talking them through with a trusted friend. There are healthier ways of expressing the grief you feel—ways in which the needs you are crying out for can actually be met.

Choose Whom You Share with Wisely

Although isolation while grieving may feel good—it may feel comfortable and safest—we know that having support truly makes the difference in moving toward acceptance of loss. You need people. You need people to show up for you, especially now. Practicing discernment is a vital part of finding reinforcement when you're experiencing grief.

Odds are you have people whom you consider part of your support system: friends, family, colleagues, neighbors, and others. These are the folks you call on to celebrate with when times are good and draw near to when times are tough. But grief can make people act weird. All of a sudden, people whom you've known to be supportive can become distant and have little to say. It's unpredictable who will act like this. The safest bet is to rely on those who have shown themselves to be dependable.

The other side to this coin is to lean into whoever may surprise you. It's not uncommon for someone you never considered a friend—someone you were merely *friendly* with—to step up and show up for you now. And maybe even more so than the people you've always been close to and have come to depend on over time. Be open to accepting the kindness that is extended to you, no matter who it comes from. Life is funny like that and creative in showing us there are endless ways of being supported and cared for. And sometimes it shows that new friends are waiting in the wings to greet us and tend to our hearts.

Fight Grief Isolation

No one understands what you're going through, you say. No one gets what this is like. No one could possibly know the sheer trauma of holding such a heavy loss, you repeat over and over again to yourself. And so you bundle yourself into a cocoon, hidden away from the rest of the world. You stop returning phone calls and emails. You ward off everyone's attempt to help—perhaps because the initial overtures were disappointing or even hurtful. You become distant, even from those you were once close to. You're tired of having to be the bigger person while others stumble all over themselves in ways that end up not being helpful. You'd rather be alone. You'd rather wait this grief thing out—until the pain simmers no more—in solitude.

Grief isolation. Many of us choose to be alone, as isolating as it may be, because being in community is too exhausting. And while this strategy may seem to be a good option in the short term, in the long term its effects can prove detrimental to the healing that grieving demands.

Take your alone time when you need it. But also push yourself to let others in too. Find the balance for what feels right for you. You may find that you have to talk yourself into allowing others to get close to you during this time. Don't be surprised when that resistance shows itself; start to expect a reluctance to engage and come up with a plan for pushing back against it. Sometimes what you need is hard to accept. And you need people now. More than you know. You need people for reasons your alone self could never provide.

The following is a list of questions that will help you evaluate whether you are opting for grief isolation versus connecting with others:

1. Why do I want to stay home alone?

2. Was I initially excited about seeing someone or speaking with them, then later talked myself out of our plans? Maybe for reasons I can't articulate?

3. Was today a hard grief day and does it feel easier to keep to myself?

4. Have I felt lacking in support and care from others recently?

5. What end will choosing to keep to myself in this moment meet?

6. How will I feel later having made this decision now?

Whenever you're in doubt, revisit these questions to determine where your motivations lie.

Plan for Loss Anniversaries in Advance

The day will come when your loss reaches a milestone: the first anniversary...a marker of what used to be but no longer is. Loss anniversaries are hard to predict. You might find yourself bracing for its arrival, tinged with anxiety, and then when the day comes it's perfectly fine. Or you expect it to be just another day, but instead spend it feeling numb, sad, or full of disbelief—as if you're revisiting the ghosts of what grief used to be when it was still new, still fresh.

The best way to avoid being surprised, no matter which emotional direction a loss anniversary may go in, is to be prepared. Plan ahead. Don't wait for the day to come and not have an idea of what you'd like to be doing. Traveling is an option for some—taking a "griefcation" to a place that surrounds you with peace or provides some warmth in relation to your loss. Blocking off the day to be alone is ideal for others. You might spend this day in solitude laughing, reminiscing, crying, eating comforting foods, and binge-watching movies or TV.

Others choose to spend time with loved ones, holding a memorial service to honor a loss anniversary, especially if the loss in question is a death. The bereaved gather in a home or public space, share memories of the loved one they've lost, and pledge to do something joyful in their memory. This could be an inspired action, the creation of a scholarship fund in their name, or donating funds to a cause the person in question cared about.

A project in memory of your loss can be another way to commemorate. This requires more premeditation than some of the other options. You'll want to think about what you want to do in the long term, or what you want to create. If it's an art project, do you have the materials on hand to create what you envision? If it's some other charitable cause, have you contacted those who could help organize the event or rallied up other loved ones who might be honored or interested in participating?

Think carefully through all the details. Ensure whatever project you embark on comes from the heart and is aligned with pure intentions.

There's no right or wrong way to spend a loss anniversary. But it's best to think ahead, lest you find yourself on that day overwhelmed and ill-equipped to deal with how you feel. Giving it some thought ensures it can become a day wrapped in protection, one that you can comfortably manage, despite whatever feelings the day brings up, in a safe environment for emotional expression.

Elevate the Self-Care

You should also consider sharing your plans with those close to you so they know in advance how to support you on those days.

Forgive Yourself to Shake Off Blame and Regret

When we encounter loss of any kind, it's easy to veer into self-blame. And it's easy for that self-blame to act as a bridge to a laundry list of regrets. We may ruminate, playing over and over again in our heads all the things we could've done differently—how we could've cherished and valued what we lost before it was taken away from us, or anticipated the loss and avoided it entirely. And while contemplating past decisions and moments where you weren't as present is a valid thing to do, obsessing over regrets and what-ifs can be particularly damaging when you're grieving.

Because the thing about loss is, we really can't undo the voids we've been left with. We can't untangle the knots of pain that those losses have made us experience. There is no moment of clarity that will lead us to understand why we lost what we did. Loss is illogical in most cases. It is merely something we can expect as much as we can expect change.

Forgiving yourself, however, can open up a lot of emotional space. Instead of beating yourself up for not being more present, for not appreciating what you had in your life, for saying this or doing that in the heat of the moment, forgive yourself. Own that you did the best you could at that time. Know that in your imperfection what you did (or didn't do) was okay. You were human. Nursing regrets and blame won't bring back what you lost. Accept that.

Track Your Moods

Emotions rise and fall, rise and fall, rise and fall, when you are grieving. No one day is the same. No one emotional state is the same either. In order to maintain a tighter grasp on how the journey of grief unfolds for you, tracking your moods can be a powerful tool.

In addition to opening the door to deeper self-awareness, mood tracking can also pinpoint whether you're having a harder time than you think in processing or moving through loss. As you discovered in Chapter 1, adjustment disorder and complicated grief are two manifestations of grief that need further processing, attention, and assistance from a licensed professional.

The process of mood tracking is akin to cultivating a journaling practice. In a journal, notepad, or even on your computer or phone, designate a spot to track how you feel and provide a few words to describe your emotional state. Over time, you should be able to notice the ups and downs of your feelings, and you can then explore their causes. For instance, if there is a persistent downward trend, this provides the opportunity to go inward and identify triggers.

Mood tracking is a mighty tool to have in your grief arsenal. Being able to pay close attention to your moods can give grounding insight to what self-care action you may need moment to moment—from sacred quiet time alone, to the support of someone you love (or the support of a professional healthcare provider as an additional person in your corner).

Bond with Your Inner Child

There are meditations, blog posts, news articles, *Instagram* posts, and *YouTube* videos devoted to our inner child. Within wellness circles, the idea of the inner child has become a trendy topic to muse about. But what exactly *is* your inner child? And how does it intersect with the experience of grief and loss?

Youthfulness, playfulness, ease, bursts of creativity...this is your inner child shining through. It is the part of you that is filled with innocence and zest for life—the you that you were before the wounds of life accumulated, and you became more guarded and less open. This space is more accessible to some than it is to others. For some, connecting with their inner child may be harder because their childhood was filled with trauma. If this is the case for you, take this journey in bonding with your inner child with a trusted friend or licensed professional who can guide you.

One thing is true for everyone, however: Your inner child yearns to connect with you. It yearns to get to know the you that you have become. And you can most certainly forge that connection if you're willing.

During such a time as this one, when your pain has most likely left you feeling raw, you may need more guidance in finding joy and bringing light into the dark space where you currently dwell. And the child within can lend you that guidance through the levity of youth, providing a palpable source of happiness and lighthearted fun.

Here are a few tips to help guide you to bond with your inner child and access that emotional guidance that is waiting for you:

- Schedule days where you have mindless fun. Try to pick activities that you used to enjoy as a child. Give yourself no restrictions and let loose.

- Watch cartoons or animated movies. Fix snacks and let yourself revel in laughter as you watch.

- Close your eyes and visualize walking into a room with a younger you. Notice how the younger you acts: what they are doing, what they are saying (if they are talking), the energy they are exuding. What does this interaction tell you about your inner child and how you should tend to them?

- Take out a coloring book. Set a timer and color for at least thirty minutes. Don't overthink this activity; don't approach it with the perfection and precision of the you now. Let yourself enjoy it for what it is and resist the need to make it look a certain way.

- Pull out old photos of you from when you were a child, if you have access to these. Refer back to the visualization you did previously. How old did the inner child you interacted with appear to be? Refer to that visualization whenever you interact with or speak to your inner child to make accessing that inner child easier.

Trust yourself as you embark on this journey. Approach it with a freeness and lightness—this is precisely the point.

Wish Yourself Well

What would it take to think well of yourself? And what would it take to wish yourself well too? As grief and loss and all the mental tangles that both encompass and possess you, wishing yourself well seems impossible. It seems to be arduous. It seems to be something you can't muster any additional emotional energy toward.

Wishing yourself well is certainly not the version of toxic positivity that many may be pushing you toward right now. (You know, the people who will tell you "everything happens for a reason," or will try to reason with you about why your loss was good, or insist that there is some zenith of enlightenment to be reached if you simply accept it.) No, wishing yourself well is not dwelling in the depths by berating yourself for not being more positive—for not being able to easily find the bright side.

There is no bright side when it comes to loss or grief.

Wishing yourself well is a tender acceptance that at some point in time you will come through this. It is acceptance that grief may be around in your life for a while, or may even be a part of your journey for as long as you are still on this earth. But it also means that you dared to love someone or something. You dared to be brave, and courageously latched onto something besides yourself in a world that is built upon never-ending change and things passing through like shifting sands. And that counts for something, right? Yes, it counts for everything.

You will be okay. One day. Some day. One day you will look up, and grief will still be there in whispers, where formerly it radiated in screams. There will be a softness now to the losses you've had to weather that before only existed in fury. It doesn't mean that you're cured from the pain of it—just that you've had practice in existing with the pain. You've allowed it to teach you what it will.

You will be okay. Hear and accept this. You will be. Then loss will come again, and you'll look back and know that in the past, despite how unbearable its lessons, you emerged on the other side of grief having fought for yourself—for new life after loss.

Read on for some suggestions of ways you can emotionally wish yourself well:

- Remind yourself there is something on the other side of the pain of loss.

- Repeat to yourself, "All things in time," when emotional frustration flares up.

- Repeat to yourself, "Grief will not break me," as a reminder that you can handle this no matter how unbearable it may feel.

Well-wishing is a form of self-care that you need most in this time of upheaval and unwanted change.

Use Self-Care Worksheets

Emotional self-care should be handled gently overall, but especially when you are filled with grief. Self-care worksheets are a great way to tap in to your self-kindness and can provide the emotional support you need to carry you through. As you may have already discovered, the act of writing can prove to be restorative and highly introspective, and self-care worksheets are one form of this overarching practice.

Most emotional self-care worksheets are based in cognitive behavioral therapy (CBT) and involve concepts like reframing and challenging cognitive distortions in order to reroute neural pathways (e.g., creating healthier habits and coping mechanisms).

Websites like *Etsy* and *Psychology Today*, as well as personal blogs, are great resources for finding worksheets to incorporate into your emotional self-care arsenal. Either print them off to fill in later, or you can recast or redraw the information into a journal.

Keep in mind that these worksheets are tools. They are not eternal guidance and should not be looked at as a form of therapy or a replacement for a therapeutic relationship with a licensed professional. If anything, they are a grounding force, giving you a framework to build from, and act as a further supplement for the emotional work and commitment you're already fostering.

If you are seeing a grief counselor, feel free to ask them for more resources, some additional emotional "homework." Many professionals have lists of websites, articles, and more at their disposal and are happy to pass them along.

Make a Self-Care Vision Board

Vision boards are all the rage, especially at the beginning of each year. A vision board (also known as a "dream board") is exactly what it sounds like: a chance to cultivate a vision for what you want out of the next year, next five years—or even your entire life—by creating a collage of all the images and affirmations that inspire you. Apply the same wisdom to self-care by arming yourself with a plan for your emotional inner life.

The beauty in this exercise is that you can try the traditional way of doing it—the route that is reminiscent of scrapbooking—or you can bring it into the digital age. Apps like Trello, Airtable, or Evernote allow you to compile videos, photos, and even audio clips to create a vision for emotional vitality while you grieve. Your self-care vision board can be as detailed or vague as you feel it calls for. The aim is to establish a framework for how you will tend to your emotions during this time.

Once you've created your self-care vision board, make sure you place it in a prominent place in your home, somewhere where you can reference it regularly. Every so often, check in with yourself. Is how you are choosing to navigate your emotional self-care edifying? Does it feel good? Are you using the vision you created for yourself to ensure that your board will help you on your healing journey?

Elevate the Self-Care

To make the self-care vision board less solitary and more communal, bring those in your support system into the activity. Unable to gather in person? Try a virtual vision board "party" via Zoom or other video conferencing service.

Practice Emotional Regulation

Emotions can get complicated. They can spiral out of control and become messes we then hurriedly try to clean up. Whether those chaotic emotional states exist within ourselves, or if they involve other parties, take heart. As stewards of our emotions, this is the work that we are all called upon to do.

Emotional regulation is the name of the game. Emotional regulation entails holding space for what you feel when it arises, naming what you feel, and articulating its impact on your body. Emotional regulation will help you successfully self-soothe and effectively find the support you need, so that you do not let yourself cascade into an ever-revolving state of reactivity.

Think of this process as "emotional management." Consider supervisors in any work environment: The best ones guide their employees. They problem-solve when things come up, encourage morale, and promote those who are deserving. Put yourself in charge of your emotions, as their manager. Because you *are* in charge. You are the master of your emotional fate and emotional self-care. The grief you are feeling and trying to make sense of requires guidance. You will need to navigate the maze of all that comes up and all that is to be felt because of your loss. Be a steward of those emotions, preparing the best path forward for your healing journey. The following are steps to help you practice emotional regulation as you grieve.

1. **Hold space for what comes up.** Whatever emotion comes up, honor it. Allow it in without judgment. Whether it's resentment, regret, guilt, fury, rage, or sadness, let it be. Center yourself in what has arisen.

2. **Name what you feel.** Once you've held space for it in a centered presence, name what it is you feel. As you ponder the name, consider how the emotion manifests within your body. For instance, is your body clenched tight? Are your fists balled up? Are you grinding your teeth? Does your face feel hot? These are all external clues that give you hints to what you are feeling and how your body experiences it.

3. **Practice self-soothing.** Things like slow, deep breaths and counting to ten are helpful here. The idea is to calm your nervous system and let what you are feeling pass through you with ease.

4. **Share with a trusted person who can support you.** Once you've comforted yourself (and only *after* you have comforted yourself), reach out to a trusted friend or family member to share your emotions and elicit additional support. It is crucial here that you are careful about to whom you reach out. As noted in Choose Whom You Share with Wisely, discernment is key when choosing whom to open up to and whom to be vulnerable with. Only you will know who those people are.

Use this as a guide whenever you feel emotionally overwhelmed.

Know Your Grief Triggers

Triggers are insidious and sneaky. They lie in wait, preparing to spring forth and remind us of the past, of what we have tried to leave behind, and yet still struggle to process and move forward from. Triggers surely have a lot to teach us—and the triggers that arise while we are grieving are no exception.

A "trigger" is best defined as "a psychological wound that manifests itself in an outward reaction." Someone does or says something, and, without thinking, we feel compelled to react. We scream, cry, run away, etc. But these wounds are old. And if we can bring in that awareness whenever we feel triggered, we can find ways to cope with those overwhelming feelings.

Are there certain smells, places, sounds, or people that remind you of what you have lost? Make a list of those things. Maybe certain times of the year are harder when it comes to your loss—if the loss in question is a person, for instance, maybe it's their birthday or their death anniversary that serves as the trigger. Know these triggers. Name them. And be prepared.

When those triggers surface, bring yourself back to the present. Tell yourself a new story—a story that centers on your pain, yes, but also on the possibility that you can heal from it. You can hurt, but you can still be transformed. You can be healed. Yes, you *can* be healed.

Release the Need to Apologize

As someone who is grieving, as someone who is trying to make sense of the loss they are now facing in their life, it can feel like there is so much to apologize for. Do you think you need to apologize for the disinterest you've been showing for the things or people you used to love? Or perhaps you feel the need to say sorry for sudden emotional responses, which seem to appear at the drop of a hat—or no responses at all? Or maybe your personality and who you formerly knew yourself to be have morphed all together? You want to apologize for it all. You want to apologize away the sea of change you're being forced to wade through—forced to swim through, even if you feel as if you are drowning.

Release that urge. Give yourself permission to let go of that desire to be apologetic for the act of taking up space and existing as a human while in pain. The truth? You have nothing at all to apologize for. You are trying to surmount the lows of a pain many may not be able to understand at all. Apologizing means wanting to account for the discomfort you may be causing others, or acknowledging how the act of being vulnerable demands others recognize and support your struggles.

Grief does not ask to be pitied. It only asks to be seen, accepted, and dealt with compassionately. And you don't need to apologize for needing any of that. No, no, you don't. You don't need to apologize at all.

Create a Gratitude Practice

Being grateful—centering on the things you're truly thankful for having—can be a Herculean task when you're in pain. Especially when the pain you're feeling is due to grief and loss. It feels almost trite to think about the things you do have when your life has all of a sudden started revolving around what you no longer have. But gratitude is life-giving and life-affirming. Gratitude can remind you to pause and remain present, to stop looking backward or projecting onto the future possibilities that have not yet made themselves known to you.

Remembering what you have—and feeling joyful and glad for those things—can lend an immeasurable amount of perspective as you continue on in your grief journey. Here are some tips for building and creating your own gratitude practice as a healing form of emotional self-care:

1. **Start where you are (and as small as possible).** When it comes to change and building new habits, it's helpful to be as realistic as possible in the beginning. Big, sweeping changes are less likely to be effective in the long term. Instead, you must learn to gently and slowly introduce new things that you can easily integrate into your lifestyle. This allows you to truly accept these changes and adopt them as part of who you are. Start by thinking of one thing you are grateful for each morning. It can be as small as waking up that day, having a comfortable bed to sleep in, or the gentle rays of the sunrise. Over time you will learn that these small things are not small at all: They are the building blocks that can completely alter your perspective.

2. **Build structure into your practice.** Once you've begun those small steps of gratitude, consider making your practice more structured. For instance, some people translate their

gratitude practice into journaling. They start or end each day chronicling the things they're grateful for, either in an actual gratitude journal or in a notepad. Others make audio voice notes or even record videos on their phone or computer. If adopting one of these practices feels right for you, over time you can look back and see the progression of gratitude. And this progression will lead you into the last tip.

3. **Take stock of how far you've come.** Noting progression and growth is a crucial step in all habit building. When taking stock of what has happened along the way, as you've incorporated more gratitude into your life, you should notice some shifts. Plan to take stock at regular intervals, perhaps once per month or even weekly. You should notice some patterns emerging, and those patterns will be encouraging, aiding you as you continue to move through your grief with gratitude for all the losses you have not had to hold yet.

Centering gratitude in your life, like most other habits, takes time. But day by day, you can stack the bricks of gratitude that enable you to view your life as one filled with good things.

Begin a Journaling Practice

Pen to paper. Pen to paper. Pen to paper. It's a story as old as time that writers have often mused about: showing up to a blank page and daring it to be filled with thoughts, feelings, and dreams for the future. Writing can be as vulnerable as it can be cathartic. The act of placing all that you feel outside of your head and into another container elsewhere in the world can be freeing. Consider beginning a journaling practice as a method of tending to your emotional self-care as you grieve.

There is no one way to journal, no one way to write. Journaling can be made as individual as the person in question would like it to be. This means you can choose to journal in long-form brain dumps first thing in the morning, as Julia Cameron has taught thousands of writers and creative souls in her book *The Artist's Way*. Or you can do more of an abstract, creative form of journaling, perhaps by using stickers or colorful markers to decorate your pages—akin to scrapbooking or bullet journaling. You can also do an audio journal, recording your thoughts and emotions in a secure space on your phone or computer. In the same way that you can reread journal entries, you can relisten to what you were thinking in real time.

Whichever route you choose, make it your own. You need this space for you. You need a place to express all that comes up while navigating this loss and void in your life. Journaling can be that sacred, private, healing space for you.

More suggestions for your journaling practice:

- **Make the process of finding the journal an exercise tinged in excitement.** There are so many different types of journals to use, whether the ever-popular Moleskine or plain brown paperback journal—lined or unlined—that you can decorate with items from your local craft or arts supply store.

- **Choose what time of day will be your journaling time and stick to it.** No, you don't absolutely have to journal in the morning. Journaling at night before bed is also a great way to dump out what may be clouding your emotional psyche.

- **Bring other things into your journaling time.** Are there certain snacks or drinks that you want alongside you in this journey? Set an atmosphere that is calming and conducive to the words you plan on writing in your journal.

This is your time and your practice. Remember that and call it to heart. You can cultivate it in whatever way is fitting. There are no rules, nor is there a wrong or right way to do this.

Elevate the Self-Care

In addition to picking out a special journal for your new journaling practice, take time to decorate the space where you will journal daily, so that it is inviting and stokes your inspiration.

Chapter Five
Mental Self-Care

**Self-care to cultivate presence of mind
and healthier coping strategies.**

If our emotions are the wellspring of our being, then our minds are the translators, the processors, the bearers of ultimate meaning. We rely on our minds to take what and how we feel, as well as what we observe and experience, and apply it to how we should act. With grieving in particular, this means tightly guarding and monitoring what we tell ourselves as we attempt to assign meaning to the losses we have encountered in the past and/or are facing now. Here enters mental self-care. Mental self-care involves practicing mindfulness—listening to your thoughts as they come, but not becoming beholden to or paralyzed by them.

In this chapter, you'll have the opportunity to face your own mind in a radical way. One where it ceases to be a minefield of what-ifs, whys, and hows, and becomes a place you can go to for peace and clarity. Things may enter your thoughts of their own will, but you have the final say about what remains and what leaves. Because there is always a choice. In practicing the activities that follow, such as breathwork, managing your anxiety, setting small goals, and practicing mindfulness, you are making the choice to not dwell in a pit of grief-fueled rumination and self-blame.

Challenge Cognitive Distortions

Your thoughts are merely thoughts, yes, but some are more seductive than others. Some are more tempting to cling to. Enter cognitive distortions. If repeated negative, intrusive thoughts have become commonplace since your loss—if you find yourself tunneling down a train of thought that prevents you from giving others (or yourself) the benefit of the doubt, or that causes you to make ill assumptions—you may have fallen victim to these enticing thought misfires.

Cognitive distortions are what they sound like: when your brain chooses to distort the truth of a situation or occurrence. With grief and loss, this could mean assuming that no one in your life cares about you when you don't get the support you need. Or perhaps you think because you are sad and struggling now, it means you'll always feel this way. The truth is that those in your life have limited capacity to support you, and sometimes you'll have to look elsewhere to get the backup you need. And the intensity of grief will lessen in time, even though you are unlikely to forget the experience.

The key to challenging cognitive distortions is to inject more awareness into your thoughts. Rather than simply accepting your thoughts as they are, become a witness to them. When you think something, sit with it. Wrap some curiosity around that thought. Where did it come from? Have you always felt that way? What could be the deepest origin of your assumption? Why does it come with a certain implicit, automatic meaning? Many times, cognitive distortions are borne from triggers and old wounds. Past life occurrences may have created a truth for you, a core belief that your thinking shifted to align with. On top of that, loss activates a deep fear of abandonment and can cause you to question what you formerly accepted or knew about things like mortality. These are exceedingly difficult, complex issues to hold all at the same time.

But these distortions, these mistruths and automatic thoughts, are markers of the past. They are not emblematic of the present or the future. They represent healing that needs to be done and new choices that can be made. You can choose to think differently. And you can choose to see your thoughts as innocent conclusions that have come up, but they don't have to remain. You can choose to toss them to the side. You can choose to willingly and forcefully create new neural pathways of positivity and optimism that leave room for shades of gray. The choice is ultimately up to you. What will you choose?

Face Your Anxiety

Perhaps one of the lesser discussed aspects of grief and grieving—in mourning the losses you've come to own no matter what shape or form—is the anxiety that can color your attempts to heal. In 2018, Claire Bidwell Smith wrote a book on this very subject titled *Anxiety: The Missing Stage of Grief.* In this book, she talks about how those grieving are not prepared for the aftermath of loss in a number of ways, or the anxiety that tends to be characteristic of their attempts to cope with their lives afterward.

Anxiety is captivating in the way that it can convince you that it is the truth. That your experiences are truthful, and not imagined or distorted logic. And when it comes to loss, it is important to name anxiety for what it actually is: a series of reactions to a trauma, a fear, an undesired situation in attempts to protect yourself. Name your anxiety when it shows up and you are empowered. You can face your anxiety. You can cope with it versus spiraling when it arrives.

Read on for some suggestions for facing your anxiety as it comes up.

- **Explore your experience with anxiety.** How does it show up in your body and mind? Once you've identified how anxiety manifests for you—whether physical (heart palpitations, sweaty palms, shortness of breath, etc.) or mental (think of phrases like "scattered brain," "mental fog," "lack of clarity," etc.)—you can start to come up with a plan for coping.

- **Try different suggested methods for coping.** There are a myriad of coping strategies for anxiety depending on what you may need: deep breathing, sharing with a trusted one, tapping, or aromatherapy. Seek out suggestions online and try out as many as you can to see what works best for you.

- **Seek professional counsel.** If, despite your best efforts to cope with your anxiety, you notice that things are still out of control for you (or at least they feel that way), think about going to your doctor to have a frank conversation about medical intervention. Whether you discuss prescription anti-anxiety medications, or vitamins and other lifestyle changes, a professional can help you develop and troubleshoot a workable plan—one that makes sense for your specific medical history.

There are ways to conquer anxiety. But you first have to lead with self-awareness, identifying your own experience with anxiety while you grieve.

Consider Grief Counseling

Asking for support from those around us is no small thing. Neither is asking for professional help. Grief often necessitates that we do more than just appeal to our own self-care or tap in to the circles of support surrounding us. Sometimes we need more than that: a kind, unbiased listening ear in the form of a licensed specialist. Attending therapy or grief counseling is one way we can continue doing the work to heal. In a proper therapeutic relationship, we have the space and time to work through our losses and resolve our grief in a manner that is healthiest, depending on our precise needs. Because the reality is that loss, and how grief manifests, is a very individual thing. No two people grieve the same—not even within the context of a shared loss.

Find a grief counselor by asking for referrals from friends or family—those whom you know have endured losses and turned to a counselor for support as they healed. You can also do directory searches online on the *Psychology Today* website to find those local to your area.

For those who may be under financial constraints or don't have health insurance, there are a number of other options too. Websites like *Talkspace* and *BetterHelp* offer online counseling and will work with users at need-based discounts, making therapy more affordable. You will have to specify that you need grief counseling, once you've created a profile. *Open Path Collective*, yet another option, is a directory that connects those in need with affordable therapists in their community, both online and in-person. Once you pay the one-time membership fee, you can search for therapists near you who specialize in grief counseling.

Join a Grief Circle

Those who grieve speak the same language: the language of loss. For this reason, grief circles can prove immeasurably helpful. Those who grieve often express how isolating it can be making sense of a sudden, or not so sudden, loss. Other people in your life, no matter how well-intentioned, loving, or caring, just don't get it. And where do you go from there? You find your own people. You find people who are grappling with the same existential questions; people who are also weary and trying to find meaning in an unwanted new life. You go and be with them.

To find a grief circle in your local community, go online. Some counseling practices and behavioral centers host these types of gatherings. Typically, grief circles are organized by the type of loss, whether it's infant loss, the loss of a loved one to suicide, or the struggle to move fluidly through life's general changes without being caught downstream. The intent of a grief circle is to foster sharing and communal healing.

Grieving and interpreting loss have never been done in solitude. Since the dawn of history, we have grieved in the company of others. We have drawn upon the strength and sorrow of others near and dear to us to find the courage to keep moving forward. This time is no different. Find your people. Be among them. Cry and share alongside their tears. And heal in the light of others. Let yourself heal in community.

Utilize Online Grief Communities and Resources

You are not alone. Even when it feels most like you are—in the dead of the night, when your grief calls and your loss feels unimaginable. You are not alone. There are people who get it, people who understand the vastness of what loss and grief entail. As with attending a grief circle, finding online grief communities and resources can allow you to talk to others who speak the language of grief.

Much of our lives are lived online these days. We connect with family, friends, coworkers, and neighbors online: emails, text messages, and messages on *Facebook*, *Twitter*, or *Instagram*. Use the power of online connection for good. Use it as a tool to confront your grief and to feel less isolated. There are countless spaces online where you can begin to look.

If you've searched online for any topics pertaining to grief, *What's Your Grief* and *Modern Loss* have likely come up as top search results. These websites combine personal grief and loss stories with practical advice and insight—discussing things like addressing the need to isolate early in your grief journey, making amends to those you may have hurt as you grieved, reconciling how relationships change as a result of loss, and more.

Refuge in Grief and *Griefcast* are two other resources and communities that have proven helpful for many. The former is a website started by writer and counselor Megan Devine, who, after her own experience with loss, forged forward in providing grief support that actually consoles. The latter is a podcast about grief, based in the United Kingdom. The hosts are comedians, and they bring other comedians and public figures on their podcast to talk about the not-so-funny topics of grief and loss. Their guests share endearing, personal, and vulnerable stories in the hopes of normalizing grief.

Do a quick search on *Instagram*, and you'll also find therapists or other professionals who specialize in grief, as well as ordinary folks who have built communities centered around grieving and loss. Through *Instagram* posts, they talk about what can pop up in any journey of loss. These posts are intended to be easily digestible, reaching those who may not be searching directly for grief support. That Good Grief, Sisters in Loss, Alica Forneret, and many others fall into this category.

You are not alone. There are places to turn to. People who will listen. Look online for the best spaces where you can find support, refuge, and understanding in your journey of loss. At the end of this book, you'll find a list of some of the communities and resources mentioned here—and others not mentioned that address the grief and loss needs of marginalized communities. Use it as a guide and springboard for identifying the help, support, and community you need.

Practice Stress Management

Like the impact of anxiety on our lives, stress can also be long-lasting and debilitating. Stress has the power to disrupt our sleep, making it only surface level and not truly restful; to cause brain fog; and to decrease mental acuity. When we are stressed, we are not functioning at our optimum level. Of course, stress is a natural and normal part of life that most of us can expect to deal with almost daily. Accepting that stress will arise—staring that stress straight in the face as it collides with your everyday life—is the first step to creating healthy ways of coping.

When we are stressed because we are adjusting on the fly to what grieving means for us, it is a double whammy: We now have to manage both our grief and our stress. Coping with stress effectively is key. The Mayo Clinic defines stress management as a culmination of strategies to deal with the peaks and valleys that life can naturally bring our way. It is important to note here that managing your stress is just that—managing. Framing it in this way implies that while stress is inherent in your life, if you are intentional, you can work to minimize it in ways that don't suffocate or rob you of the propensity to thrive mentally. Managing stress thus becomes a form of self-care.

Here are a few suggestions for managing stress:

- Delegate tasks to others.

- Take a deep breath immediately when you feel overwhelmed.

- Release the need to control every outcome.

- Let the little things go.

- Avoid overloading your schedule.

- Be truthful about your current limited mental capacity.

- Be vulnerable enough to ask for help or support.

- Pause to consider if something is right for you versus saying yes immediately.

- Stick to your personal boundaries and don't go back on them.

- Say no without feeling the need to further explain.

- Break big tasks into small chunks.

- Give yourself ample time to move and complete tasks at a slower pace.

- Let go of the need to feel chronically stressed by not viewing it as a familiar, comfortable state.

Stress is a part of life, yes, but by properly managing it, you can find a reprieve and a space to function in spite of all that is out of your control.

Accept That Your Mind Is Tired

Brain fog is real. Grieving is hard work—work that wears on your brain. When we encounter any kind of loss, our brains fire ahead trying to make sense of what has transpired. Something that was once a constant presence in our lives is now gone. We expected whatever it was to be of lasting permanence. Our brains latched on to a certainty in that person or thing. And now, in the face of loss, our brains proceed into overdrive to accept this new normal. Enter brain fog.

As tired as your body physically is during this time, your brain is tired too. You'll find that everyday tasks, even the simplest of actions, now require more energy than they did before. So much energy that you may opt not to do them. This usually includes the realm of managing your interpersonal relationships: If there is any sort of miscommunication with another person that feels too difficult to manage, you'll opt to not do it. This isn't because you don't care; it's because you don't have the mental bandwidth to handle any sort of conflict right now. This is okay and totally normal.

Accept that your mind is tired, that your brain is busy cognitively churning to make sense of your loss. Accept it and give yourself a break. Give yourself the grace you sorely deserve.

Write Lists to Remember

One side effect of the brain fog experienced while grieving, typically present in early loss (the first ninety days following a loss of any kind), is forgetfulness. Your short-term memory will be absent. Your long-term memory might disappear altogether. It's common to not remember much from those first ninety days. You might find that the things you never forgot before, things you always prioritized, simply slip your memory during this time.

With grief, there are countless things we remember. We remember where we were when we first learned of our loss. We remember how gut-wrenching, and unbelievable that news was. We remember how, in those first few seconds, minutes, hours, days, and weeks, we walked around in a daze. We remember the tears we shed in those moments when we paused and suddenly remembered all over again what exactly it was that we lost. Our brains remember all these things.

But in order to hold close to the memories of whom or what you lost, your brain funnels out the lesser things. The everyday things like where you put your car keys, what day the light bill needs to be paid, and when to call your mom and wish her a happy birthday; all of these get thrown to the wayside as we struggle through our haze of grief. So make a list. Make several lists. Make lists to remember the ordinary things.

Elevate the Self-Care

List-making can happen via notepads, sticky notes, and journals. But don't miss the opportunity to use digital apps as well. Todoist is a great option for helping you create easy-to-use lists.

Incorporate Affirmations Into Your Everyday Life

More than a hoity-toity way of hurling encouragement to ourselves, affirmations can be a transformative practice when done correctly. And they are the hallmark of mental self-care when it comes to combating negative and intrusive thoughts—which are plentiful when confronting losses.

What are affirmations? They are generally feel-good statements that you can use to fill your mind with good juju. Typically, you craft phrases or sentences that are applicable for what you might need and repeat them as often as possible. This may mean writing them down repeatedly in a journal or notebook or saying them silently to yourself throughout the course of your day. Or both—whichever feels most appropriate for you.

Here's how to go about incorporating affirmations into your life as a form of healing when faced with grief and loss:

1. **Ask the right questions.** What could you use more of in your life right now? Do you need encouragement? Reassurance? Positivity? Kindness? Frame your affirmations with this knowledge in mind.

2. **Craft your affirmations to say what you need them to say.** This means writing from the heart, but it also means being structured. Pull inspiration from songs, books, friends, or anything else that feels impactful. By using sources that inspire you, you'll find that the words will resonate with you more.

3. **Commit to repetition and intent.** Affirmations are not transformative in themselves, but in the power you give them. Repeating them to yourself or writing them frequently

will help these words resonate in your soul until you notice something shift. Writing the words down and placing them somewhere visible in your home can be helpful too.

4. **Watch those mere words shift your soul and change things for you.** Watch yourself become more encouraged and less hopeless. Watch your relationship with your grief change. You may find that you no longer begrudge your grief, wishing it would disappear, instead realizing that it is here for as long as it needs to be and until you are ready to move forward. Watch yourself be fully changed through the power and intent of purposeful words.

There is power in your words and power in how you speak to yourself. Affirmations are a way of harnessing that power in action.

Plan a Griefcation

Think of the last wonderful trip you took. Remember the time you put into planning your vacation activities—the restaurants you dined in, and the accommodations you chose specifically because they oozed rest and relaxation. Maybe you booked your flight months in advance in eager anticipation. Apply this same concept to your grief: Plan a "griefcation," a getaway intended to be a balm for living with loss.

Travel can unlock joie de vivre in our lives. As far as our mental health is concerned, experiencing a change in environment can do wonders for boosting our mood and making us feel more hopeful and energized. Most of all, it can give us a chance to view our grieving process and how loss has affected us from a different perspective, removed from our everyday lives.

Sometimes that is often what it takes—a time-out from going through the motions of life as we know it—to enable us to see our blind spots in plain view. Maybe you've leaned on a way of managing your grief that has proven to be more harmful than healing. Since you've traveled and are away from your comfort zone, there are no distractions. The numbing you've accustomed yourself to with these maladaptive ways of coping are as clear as day. And because you are aware of that now, you can find a way to change that once you are back home.

This break can also allow you to rest without having to put on a brave face for everyone around you—family or friends who may be worried about you. Having a space to truly decompress can alleviate the weariness of extending grace to everyone and allow you time and space to focus solely on you, no interruptions.

Elevate the Self-Care

When planning a griefcation, think about what kind of traveler you are—whether adventurer; luxury lover; foodie; wellness or art enthusiast; sports, nature, or history buff—and anchor your destination and activities around that.

Monitor Your Self-Talk

Self-talk is what it implies: how you talk to yourself. Take notice of how you talk to yourself for a few days. Write down your observations in a journal or in the notes function on your phone. What does your inner voice sound like? Is it affirming, kind, and loving? Or is it harsh, firm, or even condescending? Is the tone gentle and soft, or loud and forceful?

Loss requires a gentler way of interacting with yourself—a gentler way of being present with your mind, including the thoughts that come and how you talk to yourself when those thoughts arise. If you're harder on yourself than you need to be—which, odds are, you probably are—you'll need to hold space to admit this. Maybe your loss has become too heavy for those close to you to hold or support. Maybe because of that you've internalized those feelings and are urging yourself to get over your loss, to move forward much sooner than you are ready to in your grieving process.

By monitoring your self-talk, in holding that awareness, you can change the voice and tone you use when you talk to yourself. You can make your tone more loving and accepting, and less judgmental. You can get the reassurance you sorely need from yourself.

Set Small, Actionable Goals

In this new stage, in this new life—in this new era that feels so foreign from the life you formerly occupied—everything is different. Including you. Especially you.

Think of loss as a vapor: fleeting, sometimes invisible, not visible to the naked eye for most of us. But loss is capable of permeating and changing everything that it comes into contact with. Leaving things forever different in its wake. Whatever you have lost—whether a person, a relationship, a pet, a job, a former career, or a dream—you will never be the same. This is okay. Tell yourself this is okay. And let this acceptance translate into a new way of approaching your life. Starting with goal setting. Use the following guide to help you make new goals for trudging forward in your healing journey.

1. **Start small.** Large leaps are discouraged at this time when everything in your life is swiftly changing, and you are settling into the adjustments. Set a small goal—perhaps as simple as doing one thing for your mental health every day.

2. **Be realistic with all goals you are setting.** Hoping to get through the day without crying once, or running a marathon within a month probably won't make the cut. Know your limits. Obey them.

3. **Don't be hard on yourself if you don't reach your goal on the first try.** Treat yourself with compassion. At such a tender time, you won't get everything right. Your effort and the fact that you are trying at all means something.

Small goals are still good goals. Taking one step at a time is no small thing. Celebrate each victory along the way.

Keep a File of Good Things and Good Memories

Holding on to the good is hard. When you are grieving, when the losses start to pile up one by one, seeing the good takes tremendous emotional strength and courage. So much emotional strength and courage that for most people, making the decision to hold on to what's good falls by the wayside. After all, you are trying to survive. You are trying to reimagine your life in a way that is not defined by the losses that made your reality crumble and left you feeling sad and lonely.

But remembering the good, counting the joys, has to be a decision—an intent and action that you reach for time and time again, even if it feels silly. This is especially important while grieving, because it is in those bad moments—when withdrawing into yourself would be the most comfortable thing to do—that you need a lifeline to something brighter. Something that is warmer, more lovely, and more comforting. Keeping an ongoing file of the good things and good memories, especially as they relate to your loss, can be one transformative way of creating this lifeline. Keeping these bright spots in the forefront of your mind makes it easier, perhaps even instinctual, to reach for them time and time again.

Here are some suggestions for turning this concept from abstract to tangible:

- **Cull through positive and encouraging text messages, emails, and social media posts.** Screenshot these and create a "Joy file" folder on your phone. Whenever someone writes something kind to you, showing up in your time of need, screenshot that moment of exemplary support and save it to your folder. Look here when you need a pick-me-up or a reminder that people care and that you are not completely alone in your grief.

- **Go through physical items that conjure up good energy.** Plane tickets, concert ticket stubs, or printed photos— gather all these and put them in a box and label it accordingly. Here's another place to look for reminders of the good.

- **Gather items that specifically remind you of that person (if your loss is a person).** You'll need this box of items when you want to connect with your person in the moments when you miss them most. Items they gave you or that belonged to them could act as a warming reassurance that their presence in your life is forever felt.

It is work to remember that you are indeed not forgotten and that there is support out there for you as you process your grief. But it is work that is encouraging and helps you to keep going.

Face What Exists with Honesty

The mind as a battleground is a metaphor as old as time. It is also rooted in truth. We know that by embracing the powerhouse of our minds that acceptance of loss sets us free.

And the main truth you must face now is that you are forever changed. Your life is forever changed. Grief entered your life and left everything in its wake transformed.

You have lost something, someone, or a state of being that you treasured. You can dance around this if you'd like. You can preoccupy yourself with mindless activities, numbing yourself with those mental distractions. You can choose to divert your attention whenever you feel the pain of loss rising in your chest, like heat to the top of any space it fills. You can choose to practice avoidance as a means of protecting yourself. But at some point or another the pressure will become too much to withstand. And all will give in.

You will give in. And fall to your knees.

This hurts. It hurts immensely. To be in possession of something, to be sure of it, to carry it around knowing who you are because it exists in your life is a mighty certainty. Security lies in that type of knowing. And now, because you have to face your loss and the many voids that may never be rightfully filled again, life feels scary.

Loss is scary, however. In holding our losses, in confronting our grief, we are forced to face the unknown. Who even are we anymore? Who are we to be in this life with less than what we had not that long ago? Who is this person we are merging into after loss?

The answers can't be known until you are honest. Honesty is seeing that there are things to learn, wisdom to gain, and truths to acquaint yourself with. Not now. Maybe not even tomorrow or next week…but eventually.

When you can balance the pain of loss with a curiosity to heal—an earnestness and courage to heal too—these truths will come forward.

Confront the shape of your loss. Know its color and how it shape-shifts as time passes. Know its voice and vices: the character of it all. Become an intimate being with your loss and the wealth of thought and mental abstractions that can enter within you through honesty.

Know it. Be it. Do it. Because, you see, our mind is a battleground and loss is a life force. Loss and change swirl, collide, and slam into one another. Loss and change are the same and yet they are different—a pot of perpetual confusion. But they are here, and so are you. Your presence offers a chance—a chance to know, to be, and to do. Will you take that chance? Will you be honest? Will you allow the pain of what is to exist so you can heal?

Practice Digital Minimalism

There is certainly good to be said about most of social media and other online resources—namely, how they can connect us to other people. But exercising good judgment and boundaries is never a bad idea to keep both a sense of balance and reduce unnecessary stress. Enter digital minimalism, which encourages you to simplify your digital life as much as possible, as often as possible.

Use the following guide to practice digital minimalism.

1. **Determine which apps you rarely use on your phone.** Which apps have you not used in more than two weeks? Put these on the proverbial chopping block.

2. **Delete extra and unneeded photos.** You probably have hundreds of screenshots of items or information that you told yourself you needed and would refer back to at a later date. No surprise here that you haven't. And remember when you spent hours trying to get that perfect selfie? You can delete all the extra shots that didn't make the cut.

3. **Consider decreasing your time online.** Do you often find yourself feeling drained or overextended after being online, even though in the moment it felt good to be connecting with folks? This is a sign that you may need to decrease your time online to an amount that feels good in the moment but also doesn't tire you out, leaving you mentally depleted.

Why not reduce your digital content so that there is less for you to mentally wade through during this difficult time?

Elevate the Self-Care

To get a more precise handle on how much time you're spending online, use a screen time app or the function on your phone.

Reach for Pleasure

Training our minds and our psyches to seek out pleasure is an exercise in both restraint and ultimately self-compassion. Grief can make it easy to fall into a habit of self-flagellation. You tell yourself that the pain is justified. You tell yourself that the regret, relief, rage, and every other grim emotion you're having right now—not to mention the foggy mental space—are all just what you get. It's what you deserve for being human and daring to love another person, another thing, another dream, or another entity. It's what you deserve for daring to be alive and love your life so much that any loss is a terror.

But you can combat the negativity, the ache of focusing on the pain, by reaching for pleasure. You can rewire and retrain your brain to want pleasure and to let that be a guiding force as you heal and integrate your loss.

Reach for pleasure. Let your brain, your mind, your psyche—your entire mental being—meditate and focus on it. Let pleasure be what feels good, what tastes good, what puts you ultimately at ease. Pleasure can be healing. Pleasure can be wholeness. Pleasure can be a route to nourishing, revitalizing, life-giving, and mind-altering self-care.

Build a Mental Health Routine

There's a saying that's commonly reiterated: "Health is your wealth." It makes sense, doesn't it? After all, poor health curbs the amount of energy we have to extend to other parts of our lives. We know for a fact that we are cognitively limited when we grieve and when we think about all that loss has come to mean. We also know that caring for our minds through appropriate self-care can be revolutionary. Studies have shown that regular routines can be a boost to mental health, providing structures that make the highs and lows easier to manage. Are *you* in need of a mental health routine to lean on, even when you are beyond your grief? Take the quick quiz that follows to find out. Circle "Yes" or "No" in response to each statement.

1. I feel scattered, as though I am unable to get anything done most days.
   Yes / No

2. My moods are erratic and range widely in the span of one day.
   Yes / No

3. I often feel out of control, like I have no power over how my mental state impacts my mood.
   Yes / No

4. The grief "fog" dominates my mental acuity.
   Yes / No

5. I frequently fall into rumination funnels, and my grief feels overwhelming.
   Yes / No

6. I've noticed that my mental state is impacting my relationships in bad ways.
   Yes / No

7. Days are long and feel fruitless, devoid of hope.
   Yes / No

If you answered yes to four or more of these statements, you could benefit from a mental health routine while grieving. Read on for some suggestions on how to create your own routine.

- **Evaluate what times of day you tend to be in need of a mental pickup.** Prioritize scheduling your self-care rituals and routines during these times of day.

- **Ask friends, family, or colleagues for suggestions on things that have worked for them.** Especially those you know have dealt with grief affecting their mental health.

- **Be realistic.** A tight schedule may be hard to adhere to right now. Instead, focus on trying to do as many rituals or practices—meditation, breathwork, grief counseling, grief circles, etc.—as possible each day.

- **Above all else, do what feels right for you.** You will know what these things are by how you feel after incorporating them into your day. If you feel energized, clear, and at peace, it resonates. If instead you feel drained, reevaluate your plan.

By creating a mental healthcare plan, you emphasize that self-care is not just one thing—it is the sum of things, the sum of many parts.

Expect to Get Stuck in Disbelief

There's a moment when you know. A moment where looking back you see it as the start of everything: a start of change, a start of shifts, a start of loss. That moment when you knew you were standing on the edge of the great mass of uncertainty and the looming unknown.

Disbelief. Those who are grieving know it quite well. It is the natural resting position for those grieving a former state of mind, a body that they once felt familiar and at home with, a relationship that has been severed for either real or trivial reasons, or the death of someone they cherished. Disbelief is the mind's stumbling journey toward acceptance. It is a journey you must travel while struggling to make the fleeting thoughts swirling in your mind less nonsensical.

Expect to arrive at the home of disbelief. Expect that it will be one of the many destinations you stop at on your path of grieving. Bring all you need to get comfortable there—like you would if you were traveling or going out of town. What would you need to settle in a new home away from home? What would you need to make it little easier, a little more comfortable, as you struggle with being wedged into this new, unfamiliar place that you must now call home?

You may need to bring some softness along to cushion the hard bristles life now has, which were created by loss. Maybe a dose of mental levity is needed too, allowing you occasional breaks from the heaviness. Perhaps you need some bravery: Facing everything you've lost is not easy work, nor is it work that comes easily for a lot of us. Being brave and courageous enough to sit with your disbelief, and what else comes up as a result, is both an intentional decision that shows commitment to growth—and one you may have to nudge yourself into doing.

There will come a time when you no longer fall into forgetfulness, and you can live without rehashing all that you have lost and what used to be. As you heal, these moments will pop up like prizes waiting to be won.

But until then—until those moments become more frequent, and the disbelief no longer rules your emotions or what it means to grieve—bring what you need. All that you need. For once, you don't need to pack light.

Here are more strategies for bracing for disbelief:

- Honor the mental fatigue that disbelief causes while adjusting to loss.

- Name what the disbelief is for you, disarming it of its scary or unfounded hold on your grief.

- Reframe your state of "stuckness" in disbelief as a necessary pit stop, one that you can't skip.

- Know that being stuck is not always a bad thing.

Disbelief is a temporary state of mental being. Embrace it as such, and give yourself the space to process disbelief as it eventually fades away.

Practice Mindfulness and Unfettered Presence

What does it mean to be mindful and to practice mindfulness and presence as a way of life? How do we achieve this while we grieve, as loss becomes more and more known to us?

To be mindful with our grief not only means being malleable and open enough to sit with our losses; it also means being present for everything else in our lives too. It means daring to be, choosing to be, trying to be present even when we are itching and yearning to return to the past, when our losses were not yet losses. Or when we feel the urge to race to the future, frantically contemplating what our new world will be like in life after loss.

But here, in the present, there are gifts waiting for you. Practicing mindfulness and choosing to remain rooted in the here and now is a promise to your future self. Mindfulness—bringing more awareness into those moments when you are pondering the past or the future, and choosing to breathe and simply feel where you are presently—means that you can be fully attentive to how loss is actively changing you.

With presence, you can bridge the gap between the you that used to be, and the new you that you are becoming, courtesy of loss and grief. And each one of us needs to know who we are. This is important work.

Take an Intentional Mental Rest

A weary mind makes a hard place to land. A grieving heart makes a weary burden to hold. The most insidious part of grieving is the havoc it wreaks on our minds and our mental state. And because loss is in many ways an illogical truth, we have to hold it as we soldier on in our lives until the brain fog appears. It clouds our judgment and our ability to freely partake in rational thought. Forget mental sharpness and strong mental acuity—they have been ushered to a faraway land, an unreachable place, for the time being.

But there's something you can do. You can intentionally create time and space to let your mind rest—to turn off the buttons of your mental roaming. Take your rest. Let your mind—consumed with calculating all the probabilities, horrors, and hurts of what it means to lose something you love—pause. Unplug your mind from the worries of the world.

Take a break from work. From life. From thinking. From pondering. From revisiting. From rehearsing. From rehashing. From regretting. From angering. Take a break. Let your brain, your mind, your mental anxieties rest. Let them retire into a quiet and still place. And when you're ready, when you have come into touch with your inner calm, regather your mind and let ease guide you on.

Shift Your Mental Energy

Pivot. Change focus. Reprioritize. Pause to ponder. Western culture prides itself on taking time to think, to let time lend itself perspective to whatever may be churning through our brains. As far as grief is concerned, this may be a helpful strategy lest you end up mentally burdened with all there is to contemplate.

Whether any of us want to accept it or not, loss defies logic. Losing something or someone—or a state of mental, physical, or emotional well-being that we once held near and dear—is not something we can easily understand. What is in our lives is supposed to stick around for a while. We depend on that to feel safe. When the opposite of that happens and we are left with a blank space in its absence, it can leave us reeling. And struggling to understand why.

The truth? There are no easy answers, or answers at all, for explaining loss. And thus grief settles in as we transition to acceptance of how our lives have changed. Allow yourself the chance to shift your brain's energy. If you feel yourself ruminating or pondering too long in the land of intellectual gymnastics, it's okay to gently catch yourself before your catapult off into mental backflips.

Shift your energy. Think of something else. Empower yourself to do so and see the gift of levity waiting for you when you desperately need to grab it. You can infuse levity into this process in order to remove pressure by actively reframing, giving in to laughter, or reminding yourself that not everything is high stakes.

Say Yes to the Right Things

You've heard it said countless times before: No is a complete sentence. No can be a firm boundary, a line in the sand, the beginning of a personal revolution. Learning to cultivate your no's—and sticking to them without reservation or hesitation—is often a game changer for most when grieving. Conversely, saying yes can be a game changer as well.

Loss makes it abundantly clear what things it wants to opt out of—what no longer feels sustainable or even achievable within safe reach. Yes is a different side of the same coin. Saying yes to what fills you up, instead of to the things that drain you of your reserves, is crucial. Your energy reserves—emotional, physical, and mental—are already significantly depleted, nearly slashed in half, if not more.

Preserve and renew your mental energy. Say yes to what is fruitful, what is true, or what could fill you up. Say yes to thinking of your loss and how it truly impacts you, without feeling the need to put a positive spin on it. Say yes to guarding your mental space and monitoring what you allow within it—what you allow yourself exposure to. Say yes to contemplating what a joyous state of mental being could mean for you. Say yes to ways you can take better care of yourself now, and provide that care in the future to others who might grieve or journey through loss. Say yes to a better now and to the great things to come. Say yes.

Draw a Grief Map

In recent years, adult coloring books have become all the rage. They are proven stress relievers and can ultimately serve as a meditative practice. By focusing on coloring, filling in the shapes on a sheet of paper, you allow yourself presence, and thus preoccupations have the opportunity to slip away. Drawing and using your hands to create art is soothing. Corralling your energy into drawing a grief map follows this same idea.

Grief maps aren't literal maps of your grief or loss. Nor are they timelines detailing how the process of loss has affected you. Think back to childhood: Remember the word association maps you may have done as school assignments? You'd start off with a word in the center of a map, inside of a big bubble, and you drew lines connecting that word bubble to other, smaller word bubbles that were secondary. Then you'd draw other lines to word bubbles that were tertiary, and so on. When you were done you had this entire galaxy of seemingly unrelated ideas and concepts that existed within each other. You can do the same thing with your grief. Caution: This process requires self-honesty.

Read on for tips on creating your own grief map.

1. **In the middle of the map, name your loss.** Remember, loss in the context of this book can fit a myriad of situations and is not merely limited to loss due to the death of a person. Name your loss; say it out loud and then write it down. Then draw a circle directly around the loss you have named.

2. **From there, draw associations to your loss.** These could be secondary losses—things that you also lost as a result of your big, primary loss. They could also be feelings or actions that you've taken as a result of grief. Draw bubbles and use connecting lines in whatever way makes sense to you. If you would like,

use colored pencils, markers, or crayons to add color to the words or shading to the bubbles. You can also color the background of the piece of paper too, or paint it with watercolors.

3. **Continue growing and building the map.** Be careful to not limit, tamp down, or censor what words come up organically or intuitively through the mapping process. Look at what comes up as a form of mental guidance through what loss has held for you within your mental space.

When you are done, you'll have a maze of words, thoughts, and feelings that may summarize what this journey through loss has been for you. You've dumped some of those things, released them onto paper, and are now ready to give yourself permission to feel lighter. And really, that is the true point of this exercise: to give yourself the space and words for what has been swirling in your mind—in order to have some semblance of peace, respite, and meaning on the path toward wholeness.

Practice Breathwork

Have you noticed how you breathe? For most of us, when we are upset or frustrated, our breathing tells the story. What were once deep and measured breaths become shallow and inconsistent. The lack of deep, slow breaths triggers our nervous system into a panic, and any sense of calm leaves along with it. How we breathe—and how we respond to triggers as they arise—is what allows us to react or respond to any experience. Entrenched in loss and grief, breathwork is a pivotal tool for keeping a sense of balance.

An art as old as time, breathwork is the practice of using breaths to transform your fight-or-flight response, often activated by triggers and other stimuli, into one that is peaceful and calm. Grieving can be rife with memory landmines: a whiff of the perfume that a loved one used to wear when they were alive; a glimpse of the house in the former neighborhood you lovingly made into a home but then moved away from; stumbling onto paperwork or scribbles from a past dream you had to let go of. These reminders of loss are plentiful and everywhere. The opportunities to panic are too.

Start with your breath. One form of breathing is the 4-7-8 breath. The beauty in this breathwork is that it can be done anywhere and any-time, whenever you start to feel overwhelmed and need to tap in to a sense of calm. Inhale deeply through the nose for four seconds. Then hold that breath for seven seconds, counting silently to yourself. Lastly, exhale through your mouth slowly for eight seconds. Repeat as often as necessary, until you feel more centered.

Alternate nostril breathing is another form of breathwork that can be utilized if grief has you feeling lethargic and brain fog has taken over. How this breath works is simple enough: Take turns breathing in and out through each nostril while pressing the opposite nostril with your finger. As you are breathing in and out of your left nostril, for example, hold the air in your right nostril with your right thumb. This breathwork technique has been known to give those who try it a burst of energy, mental acuity, and greater focus.

Square breathing (also known as box breathing) is yet another form of breathwork. Square breathing is a four-step process that focuses on aiding concentration and alleviating stress, two things that those tussling with grief and loss are sure to find helpful. This is how it works: You create a "square" by first deeply inhaling through your nose for four seconds; next, hold your breath for four seconds; third, exhale through your mouth for four seconds; and finally, rest for four seconds.

All of these techniques are easy to tap in to and try on your own. If incorporating breathwork into your arsenal of self-care proves transformational, and you'd like to go deeper, consider finding a breathwork practitioner to teach you more techniques.

Elevate the Self-Care

You can deepen your breathwork practice even further by working toward a breathwork certification. Meditation centers frequently offer this certification online, so it is an accomplishment you can complete from the comfort of your home, at your own pace.

Avoid Big Changes for a Few Years

Loss has a way of making us question everything. When you lose something of grand importance to you, there is no way to possibly forget the void it leaves in its wake. You are reminded every day—every moment—of what you lost and the impossibility of replacing it. Turning your life inside out in response may seem like a welcome remedy. If the life you formerly knew is forever tarnished, why remain there? A fresh start, you tell yourself, would provide a reprieve and some distance from your pain and its perpetual rawness.

But that couldn't be further from the truth. The adrenaline you find chasing a "new beginning" covers the fact that you are running from being present in your pain. And as the age-old saying goes, "Wherever you go, there you are." You cannot outrun your grief. Grief is to be held, witnessed, processed, felt, and used as a means of seeing your life and who you have come to be with piercing honesty.

Hold off on making any drastic changes for the first few years following your loss. This might seem impossible or too careful of a call, but it's for the best. There will be plenty of time later in your life to move forward and integrate what you distill while grieving. For now, remain here with your loss. Grant it your presence. Your heart will thank you later.

Chapter Six

Spiritual Self-Care

**Self-care to integrate and fuse a spiritual center
into your life to sustain you.**

The core of who we are as human beings can be found within our spirits. In this sense, spirituality does not mean religion, although religion may be an important piece of your soul and the values you hold within it. Spiritual self-care encompasses how we tend to this most eternal part of ourselves as we grieve the losses in our lives. When we home in on our spiritual life and the spirit that dwells within our souls, we are listening to the deepest, most sincere form of guidance there is. We are facing the truest version of ourselves that is free from all the baggage life and its losses can bring.

Within this chapter, you'll find activities that can help you focus on your own spiritual life. This includes things such as breathing exercises to ward off anxieties as you mourn, creating an altar to be in touch with those things you have lost, performing a goodbye ritual, and other ways of binding to your spiritual self. As Lao Tzu wrote in the *Tao Te Ching*, "A journey of a thousand miles begins with a single step." And so it is with your spirit too.

Plan and Orchestrate a Goodbye Ritual

The art of saying goodbye is one embedded within our collective social conscious. Many rites of passage are goodbyes in disguise: graduation ceremonies; watching a newly married bride and groom ride off into their future; and, in the case of loss due to death, funerals. As much as these practices are centered around physically letting go—moving forward and saying goodbye to what no longer remains—they also serve as a type of psychological salve. This means that when we are being forced to face what is slipping away, and what has ceased to be of permanence in our lives, an intentional goodbye grants us some sort of small permission to forge forward.

Knowing these truths is the essence of performing your own, personal goodbye ritual as a form of spiritual self-care while grieving. You want to give yourself a space for only you to make sense of your loss and to fill that acceptance with compassion and grace. There are multiple ways you can approach planning and carrying out a goodbye ritual of your own. But the key, no matter what you plan and ultimately choose to do, is remembering to do something true to you. Remember to listen to your heart and proceed in that direction. What are your heart, spirit, and soul telling you that you need in order to process this lost? Listen and act.

One possibility for a goodbye ritual could be to gather any and all mementos that conjure up memories of the loss you are grieving. Once you have a good collection of things, place them within a box or other container. Then offer kind words, love, and warm energy toward all those things and make a point of putting them away out of view. You could put them in a closet, a room in your home that you don't go into regularly, or some other storage space. By gathering these things and putting them aside, you are saying that you know the memory of what has now become a loss is very real. But in removing that memory from your everyday life, you are forming a healing type of separation.

Another tried-and-true method for saying goodbye is to write a letter. Sit and be still. Either wrap yourself in silence during this ritual, or play soft and soothing tunes. Light a candle or burn incense, if that will help to set a comforting ambiance. Then write from the heart. Write as if you were sitting directly across from who (or what) you lost and are currently mourning. Don't hold anything back, even if the feelings are messy or muddled. Don't be ashamed to admit your anger, disbelief, or even relief. Grief is sometimes an illogical process; the range of feelings you might be having fall within this realm too. Admitting them means you can work toward injecting less judgment and more understanding—and thus acceptance—for what you have lost.

Create a Spiritual Mission Statement

Mission statements are often used by businesses to cement their guiding principles. But mission statements can also be for steering our spiritual lives, and thus spiritual self-care, as a healing mechanism while grieving.

Mission statements tend to be formulaic in nature. You state what you want to be the focus of the business (in those cases) and what needs the business aims to fulfill. As an example, Nike's mission statement is "to bring inspiration and innovation to every athlete in the world." In the same vein, spiritual mission statements involve pinpointing where you want to take your spiritual life and how you can embark on creating that change and those shifts presently. An example of a spiritual mission statement could be "To center peace, ease, and reverence for myself and who I am within every moment."

An effective statement, one that offers healing in a time of loss, uses empowering language to paint the picture of where you want to be, and where you hope to land on the other side of your grief. When you create your statement, be specific in painting a picture of where you are headed on your spiritual path.

The following are more tips for creating your own spiritual mission statement:

- Start with descriptive adjectives that describe who you are as a person and your spiritual nature too.

- Combine the adjectives to create an "I" statement that you can build upon or shift to match what you need as your grief matures and changes.

- Write this statement down in a journal or prominent place where you can see it daily.

- Incorporate your statement into the things you say to yourself each day as you move through your grief.

Spiritual mission statements can be uplifting deposits that create a genesis of spiritual empowerment. Watch yourself blossom and see how your mission statement—one that you can look back to time and time again—can help you become a force of nature. Because you are a force of nature. You are a spiritual force of nature in spite of your grief and in spite of your losses, those you are experiencing now and those to come.

Volunteer for a Cause You Care About

Grieving can be brutal. But chiefly, mourning the loss of what once held an important space in your life can be deeply isolating. No matter what level of support you get from family or friends, you are alone in the grief you feel. It is solely your experience to bear. The truth of this can be heavy.

One way of holding this heaviness while also creating space for other energy to enter into your life is to volunteer. Are there any causes you feel passionate about? Organizations you could give an hour to here and there whenever you can? While grieving, your life may all of a sudden feel a lot emptier. Volunteering could be a meaningful way of filling some of the many voids loss has created.

When you volunteer and donate your time, you loosen the muck of grief and give your brain a break from contemplating your loss. You can devote your time and energy into something completely unrelated, which can be freeing and soothing. You become a person who, if only for a little while, is not completely tinged by loss—simply someone willing to give their attention. Be careful to not overload yourself with volunteering, even if it does feel good. You are still grieving; your capacity is more limited than it has ever been before. A little dedication will be more than sufficient for your soul's healing.

Go on a Spiritual Retreat
(or Create Your Own)

Sometimes we just need a break. That has never been truer than for those who are imbued in grief. The adjustments to life after loss feel nearly constant. The reminders of what used to be sound guttural in your mind, with each one appearing often in quick succession. A time-out is needed, a time-out for your soul. Consider going on a spiritual retreat to take this break.

There are a variety of spiritual retreats available that can be taken at different times throughout the year. Many spiritual retreats have a religious affiliation with optional services that don't have to be attended. Some spiritual retreats have a full itinerary for each day, while others are more self-guided, which means that you do what you want and what calls to you. Some are meant for those on the retreat to share with one another, while others are completely silent (as in there's no talking for the entirety of the retreat). There are weekend ones, and ones that can last a week or more. *Retreat Finder* is a great online resource for finding a retreat that works for your needs.

If leaving home is simply not an option, there is still a way to make this work for you: DIY a spiritual retreat where you live. Think of special comforts that evoke feelings of relaxation for you. Maybe dusting off a stack of books you've been meaning to read, or pulling out ingredients to cook comfort foods to feel nourished. Tell those in your life that you are planning a retreat and that you won't be available for that time. Exhale. This time is for you.

Visualize Your Life After

A powerful tool of manifestation, visualization can also be helpful and healing within the context of grief. Plenty of literature and guides on grief focus on moving on and accepting your loss. The issue, however, with approaching the topic of grief in this way is that it frames loss too succinctly. Loss is not something to be forgotten, sacrificing all of the memories of the good things you had before it in exchange for moving on or getting over it. Loss is to be integrated into your life, and merged with the life that is to be lived going forward. It is to become a living, breathing part of what life comes to mean now for you.

Part of holding loss is embracing that there will be life *after* loss... as terrifying and foreign as that concept may seem initially. There will come a time when your loss is only lived in the shadows, and the newness of what you rebuild becomes your centering force. Before that time comes, you can sit with what may be and visualize it. You can be still, be quiet, and imagine what you'd like your life to be—what you'd like to become.

As with the beginning of any meditation practice, find a quiet place where you can comfortably sit or lie down. Take in a series of deep breaths through your nose, allowing your lungs to fill with air, and then exhale audibly through your mouth. Repeat this until you feel calm and present. Then close your eyes, placing your hands palms up on your thighs to signify your openness to receive, your openness to imagine.

Once you're settled and your eyes are closed, look around your inner space. Where are you? Are you at home or work? Spending time with friends or family? Alone in nature or walking on a sidewalk as cars whizz past you? What is the energy of where you are? How do you feel? Let those sensations roll over you and hold them near.

Now visualize yourself moving through your typical day. Watch how you choose to spend your time as you continue to cling to those sensations you explored. Cling to the energy of how your life feels in this contented, intentional space. Once you've been able to feel out what life is in the aftermath of your loss, open your eyes.

What you see and what you feel in this exercise is a primer. It is a mirror of possibility that reflects what you can hope to rebuild. And it is an everlasting sign that yes, there is life after loss. And it doesn't have to be bad. Life after loss is merely different.

Complete a Ritual for What You Leave Behind

Trees start small from a seed. A seed, nutrient-rich soil, sunlight, and water combine to give root to something that grows through the test of time. A tree transforms through days, weeks, months, and years into something much bigger than what it started as. Branches spread from its sides, extensions of the initial seedling. Then, with many trees, come leaves. At first, at the initial signs of spring, warmer weather, and longer periods of sunlight, the leaves are green.

As the seasons change, as summer arrives and the heat howls ferociously, the leaves change from light, soft greens to vibrant, darker greens. Then comes fall. Temperatures drop, and the chilly air swirls as the leaves change to beautiful hues of orange, yellow, and red. Winter comes thereafter, and the leaves turn brown before falling from the branches onto the ground. The leaves have had to be let go. And with their falling there is a valuable lesson that we can translate to loss and grief.

Loss involves change. Grief does too. The journey of grief is about constant adjustments to what life after loss entails. This means leaving the former behind and reframing to accept a new reality on a soul level. Doing so is not only spiritual wisdom but also a form of spiritual self-care.

What we leave behind is not one sole estimation—it is the sum of zillions of things. It is a collection of moments, of memories, of what has clear and discernible meaning. Our heart holds space for what must be left, what must be grieved, what may be accepted as losses. Noticing what must be left behind and then doing so *can* be done. Bring earnestness, steadfastness, and a fierceness of pursuit along for the ride. And use the art of ritual to help guide you in letting go of what must be left behind in order to heal—in order to move on whole with your spirit. Bow to the following ritual to honor what loss asks you to leave behind.

In a quiet place, after taking deep breaths, consider all of what you have lost and what you are being called to leave behind. Grief is tantalizing. Grief encourages us, in the name of nostalgia and comfort, to cling to what we have been asked to let go of. But leaving things behind can aid in clarity and make space for you to sit with your grief.

Really feel in the moment the weight of all those things you must leave behind. Cry—scream if you have to. And afterward, breathe in your spirit space like you are birthing newness into your life. Every ending, each loss, is a beginning disguised. When you are ready, you will be able to usher that beginning forth.

Listen in Silence

Choosing to embrace more silence can be life-altering. The answers and clarity that come in silence are often surprising. Most of us don't choose to encounter silence. We drown in the noise of everyday life. We are consistently distracted by all the means of connection and engagement with others. But while grieving, it is crucial to find silence whenever you can, so that you can be a witness to what you need—what your spirit needs.

Embracing silence initially will be difficult, if you've never done it before. It will take practice, diligence, and a willingness to commit. Just like with meditation, it is better to start slow and build yourself up to more pockets of silence. To start, think of a time of day when you can pause for a couple minutes in silence. Maybe that's first thing in the morning as you shower or amble through the slowness of morning, fixing coffee, tea, or a glass of water. Whenever it is, know that you have the time needed to perform this exercise, even if you are telling yourself you do not. You have the power to choose it.

This isn't meditation. You don't have to focus on your breath, chant, or do anything else too sophisticated. You're simply sitting with silence, letting it be. You are sending up a signal to the spirit within that you are willing to listen to what needs to be heard, and you're cultivating a space for it.

Erect a Safe Space for Only You in Your Home

The concept of space—physical space—is more symbolic than it seems. Having space to breathe, to live, to exist freely in your life represents a calming energy. When it comes to grief, having the internal space to process your emotions, to rest when you need it, to connect with your spiritual self is much easier when you have the physical space to do so. Grant yourself this permission and erect a space, a space all of your own, in your dwelling.

Whether you live in an apartment, house, or condo—whether you live alone or with other people—this safe space will signal to your spiritual self, your higher self, that you can go deep. You can sit in that solace and tap in to answers you otherwise would not be able to access.

When erecting this space, take care to incorporate items that evoke a sense of comfort and calm. This could mean rearranging furniture to create a cozy nook. Or padding the floor with comfortable pillows, if you'd rather sit on the floor. Smells are another integral aspect. Do you like certain scented candles or essential oils? Bring those into your safe space.

The world roars with noise and distractions. There are so many opportunities for you to disconnect from yourself. As you grieve, you will need a safe space to reconnect—to heal and process—as you journey to the other side of your loss.

Begin a Meditation Practice

Your soul, your inner knowing, wants to connect with you. Your soul wants to offer wisdom, comfort, and understanding in such a trying time as loss. But in order to forge that connection, it will require intent—steady, sure, and silent intention. And one way of practicing this intent is through meditation.

A lot of people shirk at meditation because it seems so hard. The term *meditation* conjures up stoic scenes of people able to sit in silence for prolonged periods of time, motionless, looking like they've accessed a level of spiritual maturity and knowing that many others haven't. Meditation can be intimidating for beginners, but it doesn't have to be. Start where you are and slowly build from there.

You won't get anywhere fast if you set a goal to meditate for an hour each day. Habit-building does not work like that. Incremental gains over a period of time are how you fuse any new habit into your everyday life. You have to trick your brain into letting something in. You have to rewire your consciousness, allowing it to thrive and find groundedness and homeostasis. Start by meditating for as little as three minutes per day.

The most common way of meditating is to sit up straight, with your feet on the floor, or to lie down completely relaxed. Close your eyes. Bring awareness to your breath and take in a deep breath through your nose, then slowly exhale through your mouth. Gently let any thoughts come up and then push them aside. Return to the awareness of your breath, your breathing in and out, as the center of this practice. Remember, meditation is not about perfection, nor is the goal to master never thinking about anything while you are meditating. You are human. Your grief will surface when you meditate. The power and force of it will fall over you as you breathe in and out, in and out. But you greet the grief that arises with compassion and thank it for arriving, because it shows you that you are alive and emoting as you should be. Then you let it go. Return to your breath.

One important caveat is that this typical practice is not the only way to engage in meditation. There are many meditative practices that may resonate with you more. Things like cooking, walking outside, painting, or any other activities that are repetitive and require you to focus intently in order to carry them out count as meditation.

Meditation can cultivate a sense of inner calm and peace, ensure better nights of sleep, and allow you to bring more awareness into your life. When you meditate, you become an active witness in your life instead of a passive bystander. Meditate in order to start healing, and watch it change your life. Watch as meditation helps you gain more perspective on how to soldier on while experiencing the pain of loss.

Embrace the In-Between

Sit down in a quiet space. Take a deep breath. Close your eyes if you'd like. Then think of a long, darkened hallway. There is a vacuum of silence, devoid of any activity or people.

While walking down this long, darkened hallway, you may feel weary or hesitant to keep going. This experience, this journey, this walking, feels desolate and lonely. You are alone. But you know intellectually that this long, darkened hallway cannot endure forever. At some point it will end. But for now, you are wandering. You exist in the in-between.

Your grief and how it exists is liminal. The concept of liminality, or liminal spaces, is believed to have been first discussed by the ethnographer and folklorist Arnold van Gennep. Being in a liminal space—a space of being not quite where you used to be, but also not quite on the other side of what seeks to transform you—has often been likened to a spiritual quest. As Van Gennep discusses in his work *Rites of Passage*, these spaces are initiations that most of us can expect to encounter in our lives, from leaving home for the first time, to getting married, and so on.

The crux of Van Gennep's work is that we are always losing things, always encountering loss, as we change and grow. Along with change and growth, there is grief to be felt. We grieve what no longer exists while we wait to arrive on the other side of what has been calling to us. Those of us who grieve know this. We know that the grief that we are feeling and trying to work through is real. It is a tangible thing that we must anchor our lives around in order to cope. Many of us find, however, that we become tangled up by the expectation to hurry up and move on—to hurry up and "get over" our losses.

Liminal spaces beg you to remain in the in-between for a little while. To accept that there is another side to reach, eventually, but that by rushing your process, by seeking to skip over the middle, you miss something.

You miss the opportunity to honestly investigate the meaning that comes along with those losses, in order to make space for other things to enter and become meaningful in their place. You miss being present to your pain and the ways it can manifest. You miss being able to bind yourself up in care and receive support. You miss it all. And as tempting as it can be to want to skip over it all, to blip over the nasty, messy, unpleasant parts of grieving, consider experiencing them instead.

Consider embracing the in-between. Stay there for a little while. For yourself. For your grief. For your losses. Remain in that long, darkened hallway until you can see the light on the other end, and until you're ready to step into that healing light.

Join a Spiritual Community

Grief breathes in isolation. It does not choke when cloaked in silence, in mind-numbing disconnection, in a refusal to share in order to be consoled. No, grief often becomes deeper, more far-reaching when the person fumbling with it cuts themselves off from connection with others. When they become determined, for whatever reason, that inward retreat is the more preferable option as they attempt to heal. Grief does not want to be transformed. It does not want to be a vessel. Grief just wants to be felt. And felt. And felt. Which is why spiritual communities—as a form of reaching out to others, to either discover or nurture your spiritual self—can be an immensely illuminative way of practicing self-care as you grieve.

Ever been curious about a particular denomination or faith? Did you already have a strong sense of faith or spirituality but somehow drifted away from it as your grief touched every facet of your life? Spiritual communities can be a low-stakes way of discerning what you need.

Some communities meet in small groups to share in conversation or have potluck-style dinners. Others take excursions to different places throughout whatever city or town they are based in. The options are endless. Let your curiosity guide you. Don't let self-isolation win this time.

Build an Altar to Practice Ancestor Veneration

Losing people we love is unfathomably hard. It's hard because these types of losses can't fully be articulated or known until we are staring them in the face…when we can no longer call or text our loved ones, when sharing long brunches and dinners is no longer a possibility. The many voids we never thought we'd have to ponder become so clear, and their truths a long, clanging bell that cannot be turned off.

Saying that losing someone you love due to a death is hard is almost too easy. The one word, "loss," rolls off the tongue with ease, but the reality is that loss takes your breath away.

Building an altar in memory of those you have lost gives you a way to both continue the conversation with your beloved and shift into an understanding that your relationship has not ended but merely changed form. Start with choosing an area in your home and a sturdy table. Frame photos of those you have lost. Line the table with candles, crystals, fresh flowers—whatever calls to you. Place meals and snacks that they loved on the table as well, if you desire. And when you have a moment, when you miss them most, when you want to call in their spirit, go to that space. Bask in their love. Feel the comfort that moment in time provides.

Elevate the Self-Care

A few suggested building blocks for your altar: scented water (such as Florida Water), white candles, and mementos of significance.

Perform a Cord-Cutting Ritual

There are emotional cords tying us to all the things that matter to us in this life: the people we love, the places we frequent, the memories we hold dear. These cords, or energetic connections, keep us fused and frozen. We have to cut these ties in order to shake ourselves free and move forward. When it comes to grief and loss this is all the more applicable. Cord-cutting rituals can help you move in the direction of healing versus remaining stuck in a hamster wheel of rumination. A note: Cord cutting does not necessarily mean cutting that thing or person out of your life, especially if they have died or your relationship is on the verge of being severed. It may simply mean that you are clearing energetic baggage and resetting your connection with that person, place, or thing.

To begin this ritual, get in a comfortable seated position, preferably somewhere quiet. Close your eyes and take a few deep breaths, letting your exhales flow out slowly. Then visualize the person, place, or thing you are trying to cut cords with sitting directly across from you. This moment may hit you in your emotions. Let those emotions flow. Imagine you are telling this person, place, or thing how much they are loved, how much you miss them, how there are no hard feelings. Tell them how you've enjoyed and appreciated what they had to teach you for the season in life you shared together. Keep thanking them. Keep showering them with gratitude over and over again until you feel you are done.

When the waves of gratitude no longer fall from your lips, visualize the cords linking you to them. Imagine cords of all types: skinny and thick, short and long. Imagine disconnecting these cords that run between the two of you, gingerly letting them fall on the ground before you. Keep disconnecting the cords, loosening each one you see with softness and intention. There is release in these moments. There is a reprieve.

As the last cord falls and the ritual starts to come to a close, offer up your last words to the person, place, or thing that sits across from you. Tell them you love them and that this is goodbye. If it is a relationship that has ended, wish them well in life. If it is someone who has passed away, tell them that they'll always be in your heart. And finally, thank this person, place, or thing once more for the role they played in your life.

Open your eyes. Sit with the moment for a while. What feelings came up? How do you feel now? Heavier or softer? Forlorn or at peace? Spend some time reflecting or journaling to capture what you feel so that you can revisit this moment when in any moment of need. Know that this ritual can be repeated to facilitate your healing and moving forward.

Elevate the Self-Care

To set ambiance for this ritual, play soothing music. A cushy floor pillow for under your behind is also ideal.

Be Open to Dream Visitations

The people we allow to enter our lives and remain, the places we equate with being spaces of belonging, the states of being where we feel balanced and most in touch with our inner equilibrium—all these entities stand to be a consequence of the disconnection characteristic of loss, whether through the potential to lose them or to be fundamentally altered by the grief of loss. When we love, our subconscious knows the stakes. And in our resting state during grief, when we sleep or choose to rest our weary minds, bodies, and hearts, magic happens. Magic in the form of dream visitations.

Ghosts, spirits, and the like can sound eerie. To be in the presence of something that imitates humanness, yet has real limits in how it interacts with us, can be frightening. But don't be scared: Dream visitations are a sign that you are spiritually in touch. They are a sign that there is a part of you that is attempting to form connections with your loss. And that within your psyche, there are energetic ties to what is important to you, regardless of whether it is something you lost.

Dream visitations can occur when a loved one dies. In those dreams, you can see the person laughing, talking, and moving about as though they were still alive. If a state of being is the loss in question, your visitation might involve you embodying that state of being, e.g., being joyful, carefree, and/or centered. If the loss is that of a place or a thing, you may find yourself in that place or with that thing again like it was never lost.

Do not be afraid. Stay open.

Be open to channeling these spiritual connections. Within all of us is a spiritual being trying to be active—trying to show up to us and prove that there is more beyond this human realm that we live in. When faced with a dream visitation, know that you are healing. Know that you are connecting. Know that your spirituality is active and wants to foster a more vibrant relationship with you. And take heart and know that grief cannot stop or dull this spiritual force.

Tips for fostering dream visitations and keeping the good energy going:

- Mist your bedroom with a lavender essential oil spray or sprinkle a few droplets on your pillowcase to promote restful sleep.

- Place crystals near your bed that help promote restfulness.

- Ensure your bedroom is dark enough with blackout curtains or an eye mask.

- Consider purchasing a sound machine or white noise machine to dull outside noises if you live in a noisy area or with other people.

- Practice yoga or some other soothing movement exercise before bed to help you wind down.

- Take a few droplets of CBD tincture or melatonin tablets before bed.

- Sip chamomile or other soothing herbal teas before bed.

Your spiritual connections want to grow—want to give you life. Let them.

Explore Your Spiritual Roots

Deep within the forest, the trees, both those seen and unseen, have lives and stories. The branches can tell tales of how they've weathered through many storms, through the blows of life and the seasons that have come and gone. And the boughs, patterned and rough in their might, speak to the temerity of what it means to fight, to live, to truly be alive and participate in the circle of life.

Perhaps the most profound attribute of these trees, of these living agents of stories, are their roots. Some of the roots bristle past the surface, thick and tangled enough for us to trip over. And beneath the ground is a complex network of more roots, deeper and broader than what any of us could possibly imagine. Roots keep the tree anchored in what it has come to know itself to be, and how it will continue to exist. Without roots, the trees have nothing. And without thinking about your own spiritual roots, owning your spirituality alongside your grief can be hard.

Take the time to gingerly look within. What *are* your spiritual roots? Maybe you grew up in a religious family, where attending services and fellowshipping with other believers was an ardent part of your childhood. Or perhaps you had none of that at all but cultivated a quiet, yet fierce belief in something bigger out there, guiding you along. Whatever those roots are, honor them: Call them out and use them as a foundation for nourishing your spiritual self.

Read Spiritual Texts

Speak to a believer of almost any faith, and you're likely to hear about the wealth of wisdom—and the immense amount of comfort—their holy book offers them. They read it, they study it, they look to it for answers when the world around them seems to not make sense… like when they are grieving and the pain of loss grips their spirits, refusing to loosen its hold.

Christians have the Holy Bible. Muslims have the Quran. Aside from being looked at as instructive texts, they are considered by some to be a form of literature: important works to read and then later reflect on, like an acclaimed novel or nonfiction book.

Now in your time of grief, in your time of weeping and mourning, read spiritual texts for enlightenment and comfort. Don't stop at the commonly touted books like those just mentioned either. Dare to read other books that folks have come to rely on in hard and spiritually challenging times. You can figure out what these books are through either an Internet search or by asking for recommendations from friends, family, colleagues, or other people you respect.

Books hold the key to understanding and, in the case of grief, a glimmer of hope of what grief can mean and how it can make us stronger. Spiritual texts can be the light along your path through loss.

Tap In to Your Soul's Needs

Back in 2012, blogger, inspirational speaker, spiritual seeker, and entrepreneur Danielle LaPorte released one of her most popular books, *The Desire Map: A Guide to Creating Goals with Soul*. Essentially a soul-planning program, *The Desire Map* helps others unlock their passions on a holistic level, allowing them to find within themselves answers to what it is they truly want.

And yes, if you're thinking back to the mental self-care portion of this book, this title might sound similar. *The Desire Map* and Danielle's approach is less about practicality and being strategic, and more about tuning in to yourself on an intuitive and spiritual level. It involves tapping in to your gut's resonance—things that you simply know deep down and don't have to think or find your way through to accept.

Grief is a catalyzing force. But it is so much more when it comes to our spiritual selves and our spiritual natures. When we have been wrung dry, when the loss of those things that felt like monumental presences and structures in our lives eviscerates us, finding internal guidance can feel like an aimless pursuit. How can you possibly know what direction you are headed in next, what direction your soul wants to go, if all of you is drowning in the pain of loss? It's a good question, one that doesn't have an easy or immediate answer. But those answers are ones that *can* come if you are patient and erect the space for them—and the guidance that they ultimately are—to come.

The Desire Map works like this: You steadily work toward getting to your core desired feelings. You are uncovering how you want the tenets of livelihood and lifestyle, body and wellness, creativity and learning, relationships and society, and essence and spirituality to feel once they are in alignment with who you know yourself to be.

You can adapt this process to what your soul, your spiritual self, needs in your time of grief specifically. On a sheet of paper, draw four quadrants. Take a few deep breaths in through your nose and exhale through your mouth. Without thinking, without pondering or planning, write down what comes up. These are your instincts. These are your North Star. These are the spaces where you can orient yourself— where you can look to go, to be, to breathe.

Chant Rhythmic Mantras

That mantras are powerful is a well-known fact in yoga and other spiritual circles. Another well-known fact is that mantras are particularly impactful when they are chanted repetitively. Chanting mantras originated in the South Asian country of India—which is also the birthplace of yoga. Mantras are similar to affirmations, as they are sacred words, sounds, or even short phrases that one can repeat in order to center themselves.

In a 2018 piece for *Yoga Journal*, writer Susan Moran goes into detail about mantras, informing readers as to what they are, and precisely *why* they can have both a healing and calming effect on those who incorporate them into their lives. Mantras are done in either a comfortable seated position or lying down. You say the mantra either out loud or silently, once when you inhale through your nose, and a second time when you exhale through your mouth.

Chanting mantras can be a great centering exercise for those who are grieving and looking to tap in to more spiritual self-care. To add this practice into your self-care arsenal, start by choosing an affirmation word, or group of words, that resonates with you. These can be kind and encouraging words a friend once offered up to you, what you may have gleaned from a spiritual text, and so on. You can choose to repeat these words out loud or silently to yourself. The key is to tune in to what feels right for you. If you start to feel a sense of calm similar to the feeling you have when you meditate, then you're on the right track.

Connect with Your Spirit Guides

There are people waiting to hear from us—wanting to connect *with* us and to impart *to* us their love, wisdom, grace, and guidance. These are spirit guides. If we are in touch with our spiritual selves, they float in and out of our lives. As you are nestled within your grief, now is a pivotal and special time to connect with them—or reconnect, if a relationship has already been forged in the past.

The best way to connect with your spirit guides is to listen. Really listen and create space in your life—ideally your spiritual life—in order to be open enough to hear what is coming in. This is where the guidance in the Listen in Silence activity earlier in this chapter can be particularly helpful. Seek out silence to give spirit guides the chance to speak to you.

Some people talk about how they can't connect with their spirit guides, that the spirit guides won't speak to them. But spirit guides don't beg to be heard. They won't hound you to hear what they have to say either. Rather, they enter into those spaces that aren't already full of distractions and noise. If silence is a pillar in your spiritual life and spiritual self-care, they will enter. They will come to you as gently and effortlessly as the morning breeze.

Reclaim the Parts of Your Spirit That Have Been Broken

Like a twig snapping with sudden violence as someone steps on it, loss may have broken you. Loss and grief may have shocked you, shaken you, rattled you out of everything you knew yourself to be. Through the disbelief; through the shock; through all the little tasks, shifts, and changes you encounter on autopilot, you feel broken. Broken in spirit, broken in faith, broken in hope, and broken in the will to see into the future and accept that the best is yet to come.

Broken. Broken is you. Brokenness is the state of where you are now. And being broken, existing in that space, is not uncommon for those who grieve. But there is hope if you are ready to claim it. Are you willing to start calling back parts of your spirit, of your essential nature, that grief and loss may have robbed from you?

You know what loss has taken from you. You know the exact ways in which it has forced you to change. You know what you may have been capable of on a spiritual level before, but now that feels impossible and unreachable. You know what that level is. You can call back your spirit, nourishing it until it reverts to what it used to be. All you need is inner authority and the will to regather the broken pieces, to rebuild them in a wiser, possibly different shape.

Call those things back. Like old friends who have been lost or drifted apart due to the inevitable nature of time, you can reconnect. You can stake claim to what was. You can be in possession of the you that you know yourself to be. You can grasp an even stronger, surer, and centered you.

Read on for deeper reflection questions to guide this inner exploration.

1. What in your life has loss and grief broken? Name these things in as much detail as possible. Write a list if you need to.

2. In what ways has this brokenness shown itself to you? Provide examples.

3. How do you envision being made whole again? What would that look like? What would it feel like?

4. Think about people who embody the spirit you would like to have beyond brokenness. These can be people within your inner circle or those within popular culture.

5. Envision yourself filled in spirit, following the role models you identified in the previous step. In what ways can you put your own special touch on the person you want to embody in this new season of life after loss?

Be bold in calling forth the forgotten and lost pieces of you. Be bold, resolute, direct, and strong.

Experience the Essence of Sound Bowls

To those who are unfamiliar, sound bowls (also called "singing bowls") are frosted, opaque bowls. They are cylindrical spheres that are similar to vessels used for houseplants. They aren't like the domed mixing bowls that are seen in any kitchen—the bowls you toss salad in or use for mixing cake ingredients. Beyond appearance, sound bowls are a healing modality and a beautiful way to incorporate spiritual healing and rejuvenation into your self-care. A sound bowl is "played" by running a wand or mallet around its perimeter, creating a vibration. This vibration emits sounds that can be calming and soothing. Usually during sound bowl meditations there are mantras or affirmations repeated to encourage further reflection.

Grief can be overwhelming. Loss can spread to touch uncharted aspects of our lives. Our spiritual lives are certainly not unaffected, whether we had a strong and vibrant one before our loss, or one that was relatively nonexistent. We have to contend with the shifts that come our way. And sound bowls are one way to do this. As you focus on the vibrations created when the mallet meets the bowl, other thoughts and feelings are able to slip away. In their place, calm and relaxation can enter.

There are a few ways you can begin meditating with sound bowls. The first is to find a practitioner who holds in-person sound bowl classes in a studio. Class members come into the same space and sit quietly while the bowls are played.

Another way to experience the healing of sound bowls is to find an online practitioner via *YouTube*. Search for sound bowl meditations for grief and loss specifically. Be open to the experience. For beginners, the first time can be overwhelming or seem to be ineffective. As with anything, approaching it with an open heart and mind, and in this case spirit, is essential.

Prepare for Cliché Sayings

When it comes to grief and loss, you've likely heard many clichés. Sayings that some people think are spiritual and uplifting in nature but that fail to provide real and true comfort. You may be told things like "Everything happens for a reason," or, if the loss in question is due to the death of someone, "They're in a better place."

On the surface, these adages may seem to be measured, wise things to say to someone who is dealing with loss. They offer neat explanations for understanding loss and the grief that living with that loss often entails. If you have lost something or someone, you can trust that everything within the universe is ordered and has its time. It makes sense to think that if someone you loved and cherished has died, they're better off where they are now, in a world devoid of suffering.

The problem with clichés, however, is that they actually don't do what they are intended to do. Very few people find refuge in being offered a reason for their loss—a reason that is often too prescriptive and doesn't allow room for how individualized and different the grieving experience is for every person.

Prepare yourself spiritually to hear these sayings from people. Prepare yourself to respond with grace and an acknowledgment for what was said. Prepare yourself to exhale in the wake of hearing those words, and be able to tune in to a place within your soul that knows that loss is never ordered—never fully explained—and instead is a part of life and loving that we must learn to live alongside.

Look to Tarot for Deep Soul Guidance

An art as ancient as time, tarot offers a vital tool for processing loss, leaning into our grief, and gleaning meaning as we transform into the person we will be after loss. There are a lot of misconceptions about tarot, thanks to popular culture. Film, TV, and books have depicted tarot cards and tarot readers as being synonymous with fortune-telling. But tarot is not about predicting what will happen. It is instead a tool for tuning in to yourself and being fully aware of what is churning underneath the surface.

Every tarot deck has a total of seventy-eight cards. The most traditional deck of cards is referred to as the Rider-Waite deck, but as time has gone on, a wealth of unique decks, designed by tarot practitioners and illustrators alike, have popped up. Tarot cards are divided into two groups: the Major Arcana (face cards that are each symbolic of an archetype) and the Minor Arcana (four suits: the Wands, the Swords, the Pentacles, and the Cups, each with a number from 1 to 10). Each card in a tarot deck can have a variety of interpretations, depending on your situation and the wisdom you need in a given moment.

In such a time of loss and grief, soul guidance awaits in the cards. Social media is a good place to find tarot practitioners who can interpret meaning from the cards you draw in a way that resonates. Jessica Dore, who is a certified social worker, combines the mysticism of tarot with psychology and motivating words to guide you home. Tatianna Tarot is another who focuses on self-care and embodying the spiritual self, along with the wisdom of the cards.

Tips for creating a daily tarot practice:

- Start by pulling one card out of the deck each morning, using that card as a guide to the energy and events of the day ahead.

- Journal about your daily tarot card to keep track of your pulls and start noticing patterns.

- Don't worry about memorizing all the meanings for the cards. That can come in time. There are also plenty of resources online for helping you understand the meanings.

- Whenever you pull a card, ask yourself what message it is imparting to you. Are there things within your grief that you have ignored or been unwilling to face? Tarot is great at forcing to the surface things that we'd rather not admit to ourselves.

- As you shuffle the deck to pull cards, call on your spirit guides—your ancestors and whichever forces you deem appropriate—to guide the messages you need to receive. Ask to be spoken to, and expect to receive what you need to hear when you are ready.

Elevate the Self-Care

Start your tarot journey by purchasing a brand-new tarot deck. You can find decks at bookstores, at metaphysical stores that also sell crystals, or online.

Renew Your Faith in Life and Living

The Christian tradition has a lot to say about the concept of faith. Scanning through the Holy Bible, you will find wise and insightful ponderings on the subject. For example, Hebrew 11:1 reads, "Now faith is the substance of things hoped for, the evidence of things not seen."

Faith is a life force. It is a guiding principle that many of us cling to. However, it can also be one of the first things to wither and die when you encounter grief and loss. The energy required to deal with loss itself robs many of their hope for the future.

Each new day offers a chance for us to practice faith in action and to allow ourselves to hope. From the ashes of loss there is chance. There is an opportunity to do something different. After all, doing something different means we can anticipate results that are not more of the same.

Renewal is what faith offers all of us: renewal of life, of our viewpoint, and of the positivity we can hope to see reflected in what is to come. Life after loss may be a whole new ballgame. We are forced to navigate our lives as a stranger to almost all that has come in place of what we have lost. That doesn't mean that we can't face our grief valiantly and with a true understanding that faith can color how we live and how we cope.

Faith is trusting in what you cannot see, what you cannot know. Faith is looking toward the future and past your losses, knowing that you will smile again. Faith is accepting that losses come, and you can expect to lose over and over again. But you can also trust that, in knowing things and people, you are made richer, bolder, and surer of how love can heal and bind you up even in your imperfection.

Faith: This one-word promise and pledge offers all of this to you in your grief. You can trust that life will be pure again, and your spirit will be whole again too. Faith gives you that assurance. Only if you are willing to lean into it. So are you?

Learn about Numerology

As the saying goes, numbers don't lie. When it comes to cultivating tools and coping strategies for letting the healing flow in your time of grief, numerology—the idea that the universe can be reduced to its simplest element, numbers—is one ancient wisdom that holds nourishing truths for all of us. The essence of numerology is the idea that we incarnate into this world and that we all have birthdays falling within the same calendar year. The sum of those numbers equates to a sole number that numerology refers to as your Life Path. These numbers range from 1 to 9.

Along with your Life Path number, each year embodies an essence of those same numbers 1 through 9. There are Universal Year numbers and Personal Year numbers. For instance, your Universal Year number could be 3 while you could be in your Personal Year 6. Read on for tips for finding your Life Path number and your Personal Year number.

1. Start by taking both your birth month (the numerals 1 through 12) and birth day numerals and add them together. For example, if your birthday is March 5, your numbers will be 3 and 5. Add those two numbers, and you get 8. Save that number. If you get a double-digit number, keep adding until you get a single digit. For instance, 11 would become 2 (1 + 1).

2. Now, add that number to your birth year, one number at a time, until you get a single number. To continue with the number from the example, if your birthday is March 5 and you were born in 1986, then you'd add 8 to the numerals in 1986 until you get a single number of 5 (8 + 1 + 9 + 8 + 6 = 32; 3 + 2 = 5). This is your Life Path number.

3. To get your Personal Year number, switch out your birth year with the current year, adding it to the number you got in step 1 until you get a single-digit number.

4. You have your numbers! Use numerology resources online or in books to delve deeper into the significance of the numbers in your own life.

Elevate the Self-Care

The AstroTwins are American astrologers and authors. They are a wonderful astrology resource, but they also provide information on numerology. Head to their website *AstroStyle* for more information on what your Personal Year numbers mean.

ADDITIONAL GRIEF RESOURCES

Websites

What's Your Grief
https://whatsyourgrief.com/

Refuge in Grief
https://refugeingrief.com/

Alica Forneret (grief guide)
https://alicaforneret.com/

Grief Coach
https://grief.coach/

The Grief Recovery Method
www.griefrecoverymethod.com/

From Grief to Grind (intuitive grief coach Andrea A. Moore)
https://fromgrieftogrind.co/

The Grief Network
www.thegrief.network/

American Counseling Association
www.counseling.org/
knowledge-center/
mental-health-resources/
grief-and-loss-resources

The Center for Complicated Grief
https://complicatedgrief
.columbia.edu/for-the-public/
resources-2/

Mindfulness & Grief
https://mindfulnessandgrief.com/

Modern Loss
https://modernloss.com/

COVID Grief Network
www.covidgriefnetwork.org/

Willow House
https://willowhouse.org/

**Center for Loss &
Life Transition**
www.centerforloss.com/

**Barr Harris Children's
Grief Center**
https://help4grief.com/listing/
barr-harris-childrens-grief-
center-2/

Social Media

That Good Grief
www.instagram.com/
thatgoodgrief/

The Griefcase
www.instagram.com/
thegriefcase/

Spoken Grief
www.instagram.com/
spokengrief/

BIPOC Grief Circle
www.instagram.com/
bipocgriefcircle/

Sisters in Loss
www.instagram.com/
sistersinloss/

Podcasts

Griefcast
https://cariadlloyd.com/griefcast

The Grief Gang
https://podcasts.apple.com/us/
podcast/the-grief-gang/

Terrible, Thanks for Asking
www.ttfa.org/

Books

Helbert, Karla. *Yoga for Grief and
Loss*. London: Singing Dragon,
2016.

Smith, Claire Bidwell. *Anxiety:
The Missing Stage of Grief—
A Revolutionary Approach to
Understanding and Healing the
Impact of Loss*. New York: Da
Capo Press, 2018.

ACKNOWLEDGMENTS

This book, this first complete work of mine that has entered the world, chose me. It found me, chased me down, asked me, pleaded with me to consider it as hallowed and worthy. And I reluctantly said yes. Grief and loss have been my greatest teachers. But this calamitous pair has also been my greatest pain. As a Black and African woman who is a descendant of those enslaved, I have known grief all my life. In some ways, it is not hyperbole to say I came into this world already grieving all I had lost, all that those before me had lost. I came roaring into this world, scream-ing and wailing, emoting about loss on behalf of all those who couldn't. There is trauma in loss. I had wondered as I warily said yes to this project whether I would regret it. Would the weight of what is personally a heavy topic be too much? Would I be the right steward to usher forth this work?

Each word, each word-count milestone, each page I penned when I wrote this book as a global health pandemic raged on and I was stuck at home, showed me why writing this book when I did was what I needed. Writing about grief in a long-form structure helped me to contend with my own grief. By writing and reflecting as I wrote, I was able to peer at the areas of my life where grief had left me stuck and in a state of unresolved contemplation. I repaired relationships that grief for-merly had left broken. I forgave those who I felt had abandoned me in my time of need, when I needed support most as I grieved. I started to evaluate the ways that grief had hardened me and committed to letting myself soften, letting myself heal. I deepened friendships I'd let fall by the wayside and cultivated new ones altogether.

All these things were positively terrifying. When you know how easy it is to blink and lose what you love, you lie to yourself that protection is what is most important. When you shrink down to a shriveled-up version of yourself with diminished expectations, you do so because it feels safe. But one thing grief has taught me, one thing that loss has taught me, is that everything you encounter is precious. There are so many fleeting moments, and loss showed me that I'd be foolish to not grab them all and deem them wonderful, amazing, the most beautiful things I'd ever seen. Because they are. I live so much more deeply now. Grief crystallized the idea that being alive means nothing if you don't dwell in the depths of deliverance.

So many people helped me get to this point of finally becoming an author. I want to give them the proper space here. First and foremost, to my parents, Sallie and Chidi Okona: Thanks for supporting me as I dreamed big and wildly without abandon, as I insisted on doing this thing called life my own way. Remember when I shocked the hell out of you when I told you I was changing my major to journalism? You were both puzzled. I was sure—sure that I needed to nurture the craft of writing that I'd loved since I first learned to write. I needed to let it blossom and become real to me. Dad, I recall when I was very young, you very pointedly noted my way with words. That latent observation gave me the strength decades later to cling to claiming my calling as my own. Thanks to you both for (eventually) accepting that I would always color outside the lines. I love you beyond this world.

To my sisters, Nnenna, Chinelo, and Chioma: Thanks for always being my cheerleaders. You three are my heart, truly. Calling you my sisters is my greatest honor; it is also an honor to be your oldest sister. I know you're supposed to look to me for guidance on how to live, but I am struck at how each of you have shown me different things: How to be brave, how to start over, how to start period, and how to be myself. Your love has clarified so much to me through the years. I am grateful to call you three mine. Togetherness forever.

To the host of other family members—all my aunts and uncles, my cousins who felt like extended siblings: Thanks for loving me and tolerating my need to hide in the corner with a book at every family function. Ha!

To the countless teachers I've had over the years who both encouraged and cultivated my writing and nurtured my creative brain—Ms. Henderson, Ms. Westwood, Mrs. Johnson, Dr. Jay Black, Dr. Margaret Walters, Dr. Linda Niemann, and Wayne Chelf: All of you saw something mighty in me, and I heartily thank you for it.

To my wonderful agent, Beth Marshea: Thank you for being enthusiastic from the moment you become acquainted with my work about my vision, my words, and everything I was trying to do as a writer. Thank you for making me feel seen and making the quest of choosing who would be on my team so easy after wondering for years if it would ever happen for me.

To a host of friends, mentors, and other writers who inspire me—Marissa Evans, Evette Dionne, Britni Danielle, Hala Abdallah, Shayla Martin, Ashleigh Johnson, Cynthia Greenlee, Julia Coney, Gowri Chandra, Megan Braden-Perry, Lerita Coleman Brown, Tamara Watkins, and so many others: Thanks for reminding me who I am when I forget.

And to the ancestors—all those known and unknown. Those who I can call by name and those whose names I will never know. I honor you in this work. I remember you in this work. I validate the grief and losses you endured. I hope for healing for you now.

INDEX

A

Acupuncture, 42–43
Acupuncture mat, 56
Affirmations, daily, 119–20
Alcohol, watching intake, 59
Altar, for ancestor veneration, 162
Anniversaries, grief, 77, 87–88, 99
Anxiety and stress
  breathwork for, 140–41
  facing your anxiety, 109–10
  practicing mindfulness and unfettered presence, 134
  stress management practices, 115–16
Apologizing, releasing need for, 100
App for bolstering self-care, 25

B

Baths, sacred, 40
Bernstein, Gabrielle, 29
Black American tradition, grief in, 15
Blame, shaking off, 89
Boundaries, setting, 80–81
Brain fog, fatigue and, 117
Breathwork, practicing, 140–41
Brown, Brené, 24
A Burst of Light: Essays (Lorde), 23

C

Changes, big, avoiding, 142
Child (inner), bonding with, 91–92
Chinese medicine, 42–43. *See also* Acupuncture
Circle, grief, 112
Cliché sayings, preparing for, 176
Cognitive distortions, challenging, 107–8
Communities
  grief, 113–14
  spiritual, 161
Compassion, practicing, 35
Cooking meal to honor loss, 49
Cord cutting ritual, 163–64
Counseling
  grief, considering, 111
  joining grief circle, 112
  *seeking professional help, 110
Crafting, starting project, 51–52
Crying bursts, scheduling, 79
Cupping, 43

D

Dancing to beat of music, 44
Día de los Muertos (Day of the Dead) celebrations, 16
Digestion, avoiding issues with, 55
Digital minimalism, 128
Disbelief, bracing for, 132–33
Distortions, cognitive, 107–8
Doctor, checking in if feeling off, 60
Drawing a grief map, 138–39
Dream visitations, 165–66
Dressing yourself, and being, 45

E

Emotional self-care, 67–104. *See also* Mental self-care; Physical self-care; Spiritual self-care
  about: mental health challenges and, 18; overview of, 27–28, 68
  accepting that relationships will change, 78
  asking yourself what you need, 71–72
  bonding with your inner child, 91–92
  choosing who you share with wisely, 84
  emotional regulation/management practice, 97–98

enlisting support, 74
fighting grief isolation, 85–86
forgiving yourself, 89
giving yourself grace, 69–70
gratitude practice, 101–2
journaling practice for, 103–4
knowing your grief triggers, 99
letting yourself feel, 73
making vision board, 96
noticing emotions and related sensations, 73
planning for loss anniversaries, 87–88
releasing need to apologize, 100
saying no and meaning it, 82
scheduling crying bursts, 79
setting better boundaries, 80–81
shaking off blame/regret, 89
social media processing and, 83
talking to your loss, 75
tracking your moods, 90
trudging toward accepting your loss, 76–77
using self-care worksheets, 95
wishing yourself well, 93–94
Energy, shifting mental, 136

F

Facing what exists, with honesty, 126–27
Facing your anxiety, 109–10
Faith in life and living, renewing, 179
Fatigue, mental, 117
Feelings. *See* Emotional self-care
Foam rollers, 56
Food and drink
    alcohol intake precaution, 59
    cooking meal to honor loss, 49
    listening to body's wisdom, 64
    meal ideas source, 49
Forgiving yourself, 89
Forleo, Marie, 29

G

Gardening, planting to honor new beginning, 57–58
Ghanaian tradition, grief in, 14–15
Goals, setting, 123
Goodbye ritual, plan and orchestrate, 145–46
Good things/memories, keeping file of, 124–25
Grace
    extending to others, 46, 121, 176
    giving yourself, 69–70
Gratitude practice, creating, 101–2
Grief. *See also* Self-care; *specific types of self-care*
    about: this book and, 4–5, 7
    in Black American tradition, 15
    circle, joining, 112
    early, following norms, 11
    in Ghanaian tradition, 14–15
    holding, 11–12
    how it looks, 10–11
    impact of, 17–18
    inevitability of loss and, 10
    in Jewish tradition, 14
    map, drawing, 138–39
    in Mexican tradition, 16
    mortality traditions and, 13–16
    personal nature of, 11
    secondary losses and, 17–18, 138
    in society, 12–13
    stages of, 28
    triggers, knowing yours, 99
    in Western tradition, 13
Griefcation, planning, 121
Guides, spirit, 172

H

Hands, caring for, 50
Health plan, creating. *See also* Physical self-care
Heart issues, avoiding, 55

Holding grief, 11–12
Hugs, touch and, 53
Hygiene
    focusing on basics, 39
    get dressed and be, 45
    sacred baths and, 40

I

Impact of grief, 17–18
In-between, embracing, 159–60. *See also*
Mantras, chanting; Meditation practice
Inner child, bonding with, 91–92
Isolation, fighting, 85–86

J

Jewish tradition, grief in, 14
Journaling practice, starting, 103–4

K

Kübler-Ross, Elisabeth, 28, 76

L

Laughing, 63
Life and living, renewing faith in, 179
Listening
    counselor providing ear for, 111 (*See also*
    Counseling)
    in silence, 155 (*See also* In-between,
    embracing; Mantras, chanting; Medita-
    tion practice)
    to your body, 55, 64
    to your needs, 71–72
Lists, writing, 118
Lorde, Audre, 22–23
Loss and death. *See also* Grief; Self-care;
specific types of self-care
    cooking meal to honor loss, 49
    creating ritual for what you leave behind,
    153–54
    facing truth with honesty, 126–27
    feeling rushed to accept, 11–12

holding grief and, 11–12
inevitability of, 10
keeping file of good things/memories,
124–25
planning for loss anniversaries, 87–88
secondary losses, 17–18, 138
talking to your loss, 75
traditions associated with, 13–16
trudging toward accepting your loss,
76–77

M

Mantras, chanting, 171. *See also* In-between,
embracing; Meditation practice
Map, grief, 138–39
Meditation practice, 157–58. *See also* In-be-
tween, embracing; Mantras, chanting
Memories, keeping file of good things and,
124–25
Memory, lists to aid, 118
Mental self-care, 105–42
    about: mental health challenges and, 18;
    overview of, 28, 106
    accepting that your mind is tired, 117
    affirmations for, 119–20
    avoiding big changes for few years, 142
    building mental health routine, 130–31
    challenging cognitive distortions, 107–8
    considering grief counseling, 111
    drawing a grief map, 138–39
    expecting to get stuck in disbelief, 132–33
    facing truth with honesty, 126–27
    facing your anxiety, 109–10
    joining grief circle, 112
    keeping file of good things/memories,
    124–25
    monitoring self-talk, 122
    planning griefcation, 121
    practicing breathwork, 140–41
    practicing digital minimalism, 128

practicing mindfulness and unfettered presence, 134
reaching for pleasure, 129
saying yes to right things, 137
setting small, actionable goals, 123
shifting mental energy, 136
stress management practices, 115–16
taking intentional mental rest, 135
using online resources, 113–14
writing lists to remember, 118
Mexican tradition, grief in, 16
Mindfulness, practicing, 134
Mission statement, spiritual, 147–48
Mistruths (cognitive distortions), challenging, 107–8
Moods, tracking, 90
Movement
compassion practice and, 35
doing what you love, 35
embracing, 35–36
finding stillness in, 40
going slow, 35
reviewing what practice provides, 36
steps for building practice, 35–36
Music, dancing to beat of, 44

N

Napping, 47–48
Needs, asking yourself what you need, 71–72
New beginning, planting to honor, 57–58
Nigerian funeral rites, 14
No, learning to say (and mean it), 82
Numerology, learning about, 180

O

Online resources
additional grief resources, 182–83
for coping with anxiety, 109
for crafting, 51
digital minimalism and, 128

for grief circles, 112
for grief communities, 113–14
for grief counseling resources, 111
for healing sound bowl practitioners, 175
for numerology, 181
spiritual guides, 29
for spiritual retreats, 150

P

Physical props, 56
Physical self-care, 33–66
about: overview of, 27, 34; secondary losses and, 17–18
alcohol intake precaution, 59
alternative healing modalities, 42–43
avoiding heart/digestive issues, 55
building sleep regimen, 47–48
check with doctor if something feels off, 60
cooking meal to honor loss, 49
craft projects for, 51–52
creating health plan, 65–66
dancing to beat of music, 44
embracing movement, 35–36
finding stillness in movement, 41
focusing on hygiene basics, 39
get dressed and be, 45
laughing for, 63
listening to body's wisdom, 64
napping for, 47–48
physical props aiding body maintenance, 56
planting something honoring new beginning, 57–58
sacred baths for, 40
sacred rest for, 46
screaming to release pressure, 61
stretching regularly, 62
taking to the water, 37–38
tending to your hands, 40
touch and, 53
vitamin D and, 54
Planting, in homage of new beginning, 57–58

Pleasure, reaching for, 129
Podcasts, 113, 183
Presence, unfettered, 134
Props, physical, 56

R

Reaching for pleasure, 129
Reading spiritual texts, 168
Regret, shaking off, 89
Regulation, emotional, 97–98
Relationships, accepting that they will change, 78
Repass, 15
Resources, additional, 182–83
Rest. *See also* Sleep
    mental, taking intentionally, 135
    sacred, 46
Retreat, spiritual, 150
Rhythmic mantras, chanting, 171. *See also* In-between, embracing; Meditation practice
Rituals. *See* Spiritual self-care
Rollers, foam, 56
Roots, spiritual, 167
Routine, mental health, 130–31

S

Sacred baths, 40
Safe space for only you, 156
Scheduling
    crying bursts, 79
    health plan and, 66
    mental health routine and, 130–31
    mindless fun, 91–92
    not overloading, stress management and, 115–16
    realistic approach to, 131
    sleep regimen/naps, 47–48
    sunbathing times, 54
Screaming, to release weight of grief, 61
Secondary losses, 17–18, 138

Self-care, 22–29. *See also* Emotional self-care; Mental self-care; Physical self-care; Spiritual self-care
    about: new life to come and, 19; overview of, 22; types of (overview), 27–29, 31
    app for bolstering, 25
    Audre Lorde and, 22–23
    building new way of living, 25
    characteristics of, 24–26
    importance of, 29
    individuality of, 25
    inter-dependence of, 25–26
    origins of, 22–28
    vision board, making, 96
    vulnerability and, 24, 74, 78
    what it is, 24–26
    what it isn't, 26
    worksheets, using, 95
Self-talk, monitoring, 122
Sharing
    choosing wisely who you share with, 84
    grief with others, 72, 98, 111, 112, 113
Shine app, 25
Silence, listening in, 155. *See also* In-between, embracing; Mantras, chanting; Meditation practice
Sleep
    aching hands and, 50
    building sustaining regimen, 47–48
    hug simulation, touch and, 53
    napping, 47–48
    relishing in sacred rest, 46
Social media
    finding tarot practitioners on, 177
    limiting processing on, 83
    practicing digital minimalism on, 128
    resources, 183
Society, grief in, 12–13
Soothing yourself, 98
Soul's needs, tapping into, 169–70
Sound bowls, 175

Spiritual self-care, 143–81
   about: online spiritual guides, 29; overview of, 29, 144; secondary losses and, 17–18
   being open to dream visitations, 165–66
   build altar, practice ancestor veneration, 162
   chanting rhythmic mantras, 171
   connecting with spirit guides, 172
   create spiritual mission statement, 147–48
   creating ritual for what you leave behind, 153–54
   embracing the in-between, 159–60
   erect safe space for only you, 156
   experience essence of sound bowls, 175
   exploring your spiritual roots, 167
   go on/create retreat, 150
   joining spiritual community, 161
   learning about numerology, 180
   listening in silence, 155
   meditation practice, 157–58
   performing cord cutting ritual, 163–64
   plan/orchestrate goodbye ritual, 145–46
   preparing for cliché sayings, 176
   reading spiritual texts, 168
   reclaiming broken parts of your spirit, 173–74
   renewing faith in life and living, 179
   tapping into your soul's needs, 169–70
   tarot practice, 177–78
   visualizing your life after, 151–52
   volunteering for cause you care about, 149
Stages of grief, 28
Stillness, finding in movement, 41
Stress. See Anxiety and stress
Stretching
   embracing movement and, 35–36
   regular, incorporating, 62
   regularly, 62
   your hands, 50
Sunbathing, vitamin D and, 54
Support. See Emotional self-care

T
Talking to your loss, 75
Tarot practice, 177–78
Touch, importance of, 53
Traditions, grief and mortality, 13–16
   about: overview/summary, 13, 16
   Black American tradition, 15
   Ghanaian tradition, 14–15
   Jewish tradition, 13
   Mexican tradition, 16
   Western tradition, 13
Traveling, griefcation, 121

U
Unfettered presence, practicing, 134

V
Van Gennep, Arnold, 159
Vision board, self-care, 96
Visualizing your life after, 151–52
Vitamin D, 54
Volunteering, 149
Vulnerability, self-care and, 24, 74, 78

W
Water
   hygiene basics and, 39
   sacred baths, 40
   taking to, entering, 37–38
   value in grieving process, 37–38
Wellness, wishing yourself well, 93–94
Western tradition, grief in, 13
Wisdom of body, listening to, 64
Wishing yourself well, 93–94
Worksheets, self-care, 95

Y
Yes, saying to right things, 137